WORK IN PRODUCTION

PART ONE:

HOW TO FORMAT YOUR RESUME TO START OR

UPGRADE YOUR CAREER IN

FILM AND TELEVISION PRODUCTION

by Robyn L. Coburn

© Robyn L. Coburn
WorkInProduction.com
2232 S. Orange Dr
Los Angeles, CA 90016

Contents

CHAPTER 1: INTRODUCTION 7

Your Production Resume 11

Steps to Building Your Production Resume 12

How long should your resume be? 13

Customizing...14

About ATS or Applicant Tracking Systems 14

References 15

The Disclaimer...17

CHAPTER 2: THE LETTERHEAD 18

Regional filmmakers..20

Email Addresses that are professional............................21

CHAPTER 3: SUMMARY AND SKILLS SECTION...........23

Skills List 23

CHAPTER 4: FORMAT YOUR CREDITS...........................27

The Right Format 28

Credits for the body of an Email 33

CHAPTER 5: OTHER WORK EXPERIENCE 35

Highlight Relevant Duties..36

Incorporating your references into your experience............37

A special note to Veterans.....................................38

No Experience Whatsoever 39

CHAPTER 6: EDUCATION SECTION 41

So, what about film school? Is it worth it? 43

Know your purpose in attending film school.........44

CHAPTER 7: CUSTOMIZING YOUR   RESUME..........47

Why do this? 47

Research the Company and the People................48

Addressing your resume 49

Visual Appeal..50

CHAPTER 8: FINDING YOUR JOB LEADS 52

Job Hunting 52

Production Listings and Job Boards 55

Network, network, network 60

LinkedIn, Social Media and your website 65

The Low Budget World 67

CHAPTER 9: COLD CALLING............................76

Calling Your Leads 76

Cold Calling the Production Company during Preparation....77

Calling the Production Office During Pre-Production. 80

Following Up on a sent Resume. 83

The Union 85

CHAPTER 10: JOB INTERVIEWS 88

Your Personal Presentation - or how to dress for your
production job interviews..88

Men...88

Women...90

What about movie tee shirts - especially as homage? 92

The Interview 92

Follow Up 99

New Trends in Job Interview Practices 99

Test tasks..102

Safety 102

CHAPTER 11: BEYOND ENTRY LEVEL...104

Studio, Network and Production Company Gigs 104

Keeping Current 104

Box/Kit Rentals...105

Career Paths 107

Feature Film Director 108

Cinematographer 110

Production Designer 112

Editor 115

Production Sound Mixer 117

Producer 118

Writer 121

Never Stop Networking 123

CHAPTER 12: MY SERVICE 124

The Client Survey 124

CHAPTER 13: RESOURCES AND LINKS 128

CHAPTER 14: ATS VS HUMAN 130

What is an ATS? 130

Headings 132

About length 133

How do you get your resume in front of a human? 134

Education 135

Customizing - Keywords and Key Phrases 135

Skills 137

Determining Your Duties from Past Jobs 139

Etc. 142

Credits on ATS Resumes..................................... 142

Finding the Names 143

ATS Formatting Tips 144

CHAPTER 15: INTRODUCTION TO ANALYZING A JOB LISTING 146

CHAPTER 1: INTRODUCTION

This book is founded on the process and principles that I use in my work when I help people start or upgrade their careers in film and television production, by creating industry standard resumes. While there is information scattered throughout that might be of use to actors or people working in other fields, including creative ones, the primary focus is on **entry level film and television production jobs**, how to find them, and the ways in which an entertainment resume is formatted differently from those of business, retail, office work or other specialized industries. You may be able to glean useful tips for those industries along the way, but those job seekers are not the intended audience.

You will find step-by-step instructions for formatting your production resume, tips for customizing it, and then useful advice for finding work, and a cold calling "script" to help you get past the gatekeepers. At the end, you will find information about compiling a regular office style resume, for those of you interested in working at Studios, Networks, production companies or agencies.

Some of the information started life on my blog at WorkInProduction.com, where in some cases you will find more detail and specific examples of the ideas that I share here, as well as interviews with people working in the business. Most of the images in this book are based on my actual resumes, or others that I have either received or created with the identifying information redacted. I have altered the names on the example resumes, and combined information in some cases.

If you want to read the article that started it all, you can go here: http://workinproduction.com/five-tips-for-finding-work-in-film/

Like my parents before me, I have been in entertainment for most of my working life, almost 40 years. I started as an actor at the age of 16. My summer job was working with a small roaming theater company putting on holiday shows for children. In Australia, we call them Pantomimes. I have been a theater costume, set, sound and lighting designer, a technical director, and a theater tech teacher. I've worked in all kinds of theater from community to educational to Broadway style hit musicals.

In my film career, I have worked in the production office, a tiny bit of Wardrobe, and in the Art Department, doing everything from On-set Dresser to Set Decorator, Art Director and Production Designer. I've been in the office to watch and listen as the Line Producer made hiring decisions, and I've interviewed and hired people myself for my department, both paid staff and interns.

The truth is that there will always be more people coming into the entertainment industry. It is a place for people with big dreams, but also a place where people's dreams are crushed. You must truly love what you do to stay persistent on what can be a very long road.

Many newcomers are just like I was 22 years ago - people with a strong belief in their own creativity, with skills but few credits, and *having taken bad advice to heart* about their career path.

The good advice I got was "it's not what you know, it's who you know." That's a rather muddy way of describing networking. However, expressed like that it implies that you have to "know" the top people - which is not correct. The absolute majority of your job leads will come from colleagues and peers. *"Network as much as you can"* is excellent advice.

But the bad advice that I heard, and read in several sources, was that I should position myself as what I **wanted** to be, in my case a Production Designer, do that department head job as soon as possible, and that the projects would get bigger.

Naively, I did just that, quickly moving from on-set dresser to set decorator and then into production design on low budget films. But the projects *didn't* get bigger. That was because that's **not how the business works**.

I now know that most people stay within their own networks, and my network was of people all working at a certain budget level. Actually, most people's networks are at a certain budget level. No matter how large of a fish you are in your small pond, if you are still in a small pond, it is tough to jump out into the big one.

The truth is that you **tend to stay at the budget level where you started** - the budget level indicated by your credits.

So how do you get started?

Here's what I know for sure: **The overwhelming majority of your jobs in production will come from personal referrals.**

Network, network, network.

A personal referral from someone the hirer trusts can overcome a poorly formatted resume, a badly written cover letter, a lack of experience, or even a history of mediocrity. It's a case of the devil-you-know. People would rather hire someone they or their colleagues know, even if that person has a few annoying quirks, than a complete stranger, who might be a disaster.

You will also hear about productions crewing up and production companies hiring from your colleagues and friends, way before the gigs appear in listings. These are the most valuable job leads, before the office gets inundated with resumes.

Network, network, network.

Your Production Resume

Production resumes are *different* from sales, business or office resumes. People in the industry know this. Therefore, handing someone a resume formatted incorrectly, a standard office resume, makes you stand out as someone who is brand new and possibly clueless.

The primary focus of a production resume is always your *past credits*, rather than the duties of your past jobs. If you are new, of course you have very few credits outside of your student gigs, or your internships (the beginning of your network). This means that you will include student work on your documents, along with other employment outside of the field. These other things will eventually "drop off the bottom" of your resume as you gain more credits. But at least they can be formatted properly, so you look like a serious industry aspirant.

Past job duties only become important if you can show how they might be relevant to entry level film work. These are called "transferable skills". The newer you are, the more important your networking becomes so that someone you know gives you a chance, and the more vital it is that you gain high quality internships while studying.

Remember, the function of any resume is to get you a *job interview.* No resume alone will get you a job. However, a poorly written one can lose you the opportunity.

Steps to Building Your Production Resume

1. Gather your information, including confirming the titles and people involved of your productions, and your past employment information. Check your old call sheets and IMDb.com. You might need to check your calendars to confirm the dates.

2. Create your Letterhead.

3. Format your Credits by section.

4. Write up your Education.

5. Write up your other Work Experience.

6. Compose your Summary if needed, and Skills section, if needed. It is always better to do this last so that nothing is forgotten.

7. Save time later by making up three or four documents with basic customization, such as a Film resume, TV resume or possibly some for different departments, depending on your past credits.

8. Double check all your spelling!

9. Start uploading your most general resume to social media and job sites, and update your Linked In profile.

10. Prepare your references list.

How long should your resume be?

Like so many areas of life, technology has changed what people expect in a resume.

There are people out there still perpetuating the myth that a resume should only ever be one page. This is old fashioned advice based on the time when resumes were either printed at Kinko's and mailed, or faxed and spat out by a machine that cost paper and ink. Nowadays resumes are almost always emailed to Production and may or may not be printed at the receiving end.

Today only the most entry level high-school grad will have a single page resume. Most employers would expect 2-3 pages. On the other hand, just because you can send tons of material by email, doesn't mean you should. 1 or 2 pages of relevant, elegantly formatted credits will always win ahead of 5 pages of padded fluff and unconnected other work experience that makes the reader search for your production history.

Customizing

When I build a resume for my clients I try to make sure that the information on the first page is the most relevant to the production being approached. Every resume must be customized to the job to the extent your information allows. The most basic customization is to bring Film credits to the top for a film resume, TV credits to the top for a TV resume and Commercials to the top for a commercials resume.

About ATS or Applicant Tracking Systems

It will be repeated throughout this book, that the best way to find work is through networking and referrals to actual human individuals hiring for crews and companies. These are *not* usually jobs that are listed in job sites, journals or papers, in the traditional "Want Ad" way. However, for jobs that *are* listed/advertised, most of those employers will use an ATS – Applicant Tracking System - to sort the applicants.

It has been said that 90% of employers use some form of ATS throughout the job market, although I suspect that the percentage in the film business would be somewhat lower, commensurate with the high percentage of jobs in production roles, that are not listed and are filled through personal referrals.

ATS users also tend to be larger companies that have an HR (Human Resources) department or Hiring Manager whose only task is hiring staff. This is by contrast to the UPM and other department heads on movie productions, who handle hiring along with their other production duties. (It is because they are so busy, that it is important to have a clear, easily readable, properly formatted production resume so they can see at a glance that you are worth interviewing.)

For this book, we will assume that the default is a resume intended for a human reader – "direct submission" or DS for short. This is not an official designation of any kind, just shorthand for us. As always, if you can get invited to put your resume directly into a person's hands, that is the best path to being hired.

You can find information and tips about formatting for ATS in a later chapter.

References

Don't put "References on Request". That just takes up a line of space for nothing. If they want to hire you, they *will* want your references. Assume that to be so, and don't make them work for the refs by "requesting" them. Instead attach them as a separate document to your resume email, and bring a couple of copies to your interview. This shows your thoughtful consideration and respect for their busy schedules.

Your references are a list of your past supervisors' names with their job title, company and contact phone number, possibly their email address. Don't get fancy and make a table or spreadsheet. Just keep it simple, clear and easy to read, on a page with your same letterhead at the top.

Name, Job title
Company
123.456.7890
Email address

Don't be old fashioned and label the phone or email:

- ~~Phone:~~ (123) 456-7890 <<<< I don't like this old-fashioned way of writing phone numbers much either, but some Forms insist. It is old, but still correct.
- ~~Email:~~ their_email@wherever.com

Most of the time someone considering hiring you will phone two or three of your references, especially if they see a person whose name they know. Always ask permission to use a person as a reference and do try to ensure that they are someone who will give a positive review.

Here's a bonus tip: outside of academia, almost no-one will read your beautiful letters of recommendation or testimonials. Don't bother bringing them unless they are specifically requested.

Just have the list.

The Disclaimer

I want you to be happy, but no-one can guarantee you any particular job or overall success in your career. This business depends on so many factors both within and outside of any one job seeker's control. You are paying for my expert opinion and suggestions in this book, but it will be up to you to take responsibility and implement the ideas as you see fit. I am not to be held liable in any way for any results, damages or difficulties resulting from my suggestions or the book's content.

CHAPTER 2: THE LETTERHEAD

Imagine a UPM with a pile of resumes in front of them. They riffle through the pile, looking primarily at the top couple of inches of each page, and pull out a few to look at more closely. Or perhaps they scroll through pages on a screen, waiting for something to jump out at them. The resumes that are immediately clear and easy to read – especially the job title – give absolutely the best impression. You are saving them that most valuable commodity, time.

Your letterhead doesn't have to be scary or a big deal. You don't have to design a logo, or get all fancy. Don't use a special font, or go nuts with color. All you need is your name, job title and contact information expressed in such a way that you make it easy for people to call you for your interview.

The first thing I do, on the Word document that will become your resume, is hit the Layout tab and set all the Margins to Narrow. This way I know everything will fit.

Your letterhead should be your name, your job title – the job for which you are applying – and then your contact phone number, in nice big letters stretching across the page. The entry level job will almost always be "Production Assistant". Sometimes you might put the department - e.g. "Art Department". Your Job Title in your Letterhead already replaces the crashingly old fashioned "Objective" and clarifies what position you seek.

Then your street address and email address go under that, smaller. For DS resumes, I like to box the letterhead, or put a strong line separating the next headings. If you have a nice website or a reel site, put that link centered on that second line of contact info.

Rarely I will center the contact information. This can be helpful for a very long job title, or a resume with fewer credits. Here are some examples.

Robyn Coburn – Production Designer 123.456.7890
dezignarob@gmail.com   1234 Street St, City, CA 90016

James H. Coburn IV, C.A.S.
PRODUCTION SOUND MIXER
123.456.7451
email@website.com

Robyn Coburn – Art Department   123.456.7890
dezignarob@gmail.com   WorkInProduction.com   1234 Street St, City, CA 90016
===

James H. Coburn IV, CAS – Production Sound Mixer 123.456.790
email@website.com   1234 Street St, City, CA 90016

For DS resumes, I used to like to put the letterhead on each page, with the pages numbered clearly - Pg 2/2. This was in case they were printed and accidentally separated, or to make it easier for the UPM to recall whose resume they are looking at, when scrolling. Now I prefer to put the Name, Job Title and Number in the Header starting on page 2.

If you do use your letterhead multiple times, remember to change the job title as needed on ALL pages.

Regional filmmakers

Try to have a local-to-the-job phone number and address. Certainly, not all but most film, network television and cable network production work originates in Los Angeles, and to a lesser extent, New York. Much of the hiring is done in those two towns, even for productions shooting out of town, especially for department heads.

However, some local production crews may be hired in regional centers, and for Location Managers and their assistants, detailed local knowledge is a plus. If you live somewhere outside of LA/NY the first thing you will want to do is discover your local film commission and get on their available crew listing. Check and see if they organize any networking events and see if your city has a film festival of any kind, where you can volunteer or possibly be hired.

Local television stations in small towns tend to provide primarily local news related original content, but some larger cities have their own shows related to events, attractions or travel. (I don't discuss public access TV because these are rarely productions that will employ people for pay, and I suspect YouTube and other content streaming sites are slowly pushing those out.)

The truth is, except for a few specialized niches, most of the time your career can only go so far if you choose to live primarily somewhere other than Los Angeles or New York. You should at least be visiting the major cities for some networking sometimes. That is up to you.

But either way, it is good to have a Los Angeles phone number and address for LA based gigs.

Email Addresses that are professional

Serious professionals have serious email addresses. Preferably it includes your name and is without a long string of numbers making it hard to recall. Ideally you will have a gmail.com or me.com address, if you don't have your email through your own website. Please reconsider if you have a Hotmail address. If you are a recent graduate, I encourage you to move on from the school.edu email address you are probably still using. It just makes you look like you are still at school.

If your name is John Smith, and you need some other email designation to avoid the number string, make sure that you say your prospective email addy out loud a few times. Make sure it isn't unintentionally funny - and certainly don't try to be funny. You'd get tired of people laughing and exclaiming at the pun your ID makes soon enough. Try to make the spelling self-explanatory - although people can turn even the most innocuously spelled name into some oddball spelling. But in general, you don't want to have to spell the whole thing out every time. Be careful of initials that sound very similar - B, D, T, M and N, S and F.

Why is how an email sounds important? Because a lot of your job search and interviews will be on the phone. It is easier for an interviewer to remember a simple email and name that reads like what they are hearing.

CHAPTER 3: SUMMARY AND SKILLS SECTION

If you are new you won't need a Summary for Production work - for example, if you are a recent graduate applying for a Production Assistant gig. It is only for people with longer experience that I like to include a Summary with some metrics.

Summaries are best for jobs in production offices, development, film marketing, studio administration/support gigs of different kinds, and film education, most of which will be listed (want ads), rather than DS production jobs. They are also very useful for your *Linked In profile*.

That being said, when I do write a summary, generally I like to bullet the points, and will usually start with those most apropos to the job at hand.

Skills List

For most Production resumes, the skills are implicit in the past job title. The person reading your resume already knows all about the duties of every production job, so there is no need to explain them. If you were a PA, then you demonstrably have the skills of a PA. This is one of the biggest differences between business/sales/office resumes and production resumes.

However, for *Office PA* gigs, it is useful to add your computer skills, under the heading "Skills" after your credits.

Everyone wants MS Office Suite, and to elucidate your familiarity with filmmaking software like Movie Magic, Final Draft or Adobe Premiere. Express them simply like this:

*Highly Proficient with Microsoft Office Suite and Adobe Photoshop [say here if you are Adobe Certified]; Fluent with Mac and Windows OS; [any other general office software or specified from listing]; Very comfortable with [whichever] Content Management System [e.g. WordPress]

*Highly proficient with [any film related software]

*Social Media savvy especially [Facebook, Instagram, Twitter, Pinterest, Tumblr, Google+, and any others]

Note: These are general skills for PA and Office PA gigs. It is almost entirely pointless to add your student experience with the Red camera or other film equipment. Sometimes a Post Production house will list a job and want familiarity with some Editing or remixing gear - so then you have the happy opportunity to elucidate your familiarity with it from college.

You might want to mention that you have a reliable car and clean driving record.

On the next couple of pages are some examples.

Summary

- Over 9 years' experience in Casting and Talent, and as a Production Coordinator, and Project Manager, in broadcasting, including for Networks and Cable, and online media platforms
- Previous assistant experience with individuals and within organizations
- Outstanding organizational skills with proven experience working with actors and managers
- Strong production office experience, with strong general office skills including filing, data entry
- Proven experience with budgeting, able to manage schedules and maintain calendars
- Highly PC proficient especially with Microsoft Office Suite including Word, Excel, and Outlook; proficient with Mac OS, Central Desktop, Prezi, Final Draft, Movie Magic, Internet Explorer; Good knowledge of cloud computing including Dropbox
- Experienced with digital casting services such as Breakdown Express and LA Casting; very quick study of new Apps and software programs
- Outstanding written and verbal communicator including by phone, email, and in person; excellent presentation skills and good ability to create expense reports; strong attention to detail
- Excellent multi-tasking skills with strong ability to prioritize and work to deadlines; outstanding time management skills; thrives in fast-paced environments; proactive self-starter with seeking attitude

Here is a detailed summary for someone with a great deal of experience in Casting, with an emphasis on Production Office skills. This is the kind of summary that would normally be in response to a job lising.

Summary

- 25+ years as a Producer of feature films & television, and an Executive in production and development, both as a freelance contractor, and as a stakeholder in independent production entities
- Created budgets and production schedules for projects ranging from under $100,000 to over $50Million
  - Hired and managed crews from between 50 to over 120 people
- Outstanding cross-function communicator and negotiator
- Innovative problem solver
- Deep experience with international film shoots with multiple locations in multiple countries
  - Negotiated contracts and vendor services on numerous occasions in foreign shooting locales with corporate, governmental and civic organizations
  - Fluent bilingual English/German

The very strong experience of this film worker is immediately obvious, although again, the use of this resume would be for a listed Studio or Production Company position or for their Linked In profile.

Most people with this level of experience would be using a bio as their primary job seeking document, would be hired through contacts and referrals, and probably head-hunted by a recruiter for Production company VP and management jobs.

CHAPTER 4: FORMAT YOUR CREDITS

Some years ago, I designed the set for a charity awards show here in Los Angeles. One of the presenters was Mr. Martin Scorsese. I met him briefly back stage while he was waiting to go on, rather endearingly nervous. We started to chat. He told me that before a shoot started he sometimes had a nightmare where he arrived on the set to start in the morning, only to find nothing was ready and there was no-one to work. In his bad dream, he had to run the camera, hang the lights, push the dolly and "do everything" himself. I said, "That sounds like the movies I work on" and he laughed.

The entry level job is always Production Assistant (PA). They are the people you get to "do anything". Many departments have PAs, and currently, they are not a Union position. PAs may or may not get an actual line in the film's end-credit crawl. In the UK PAs are called Runners, although in the US film business, that is a subset of PA, whose job is errands. There are levels and status to PAs too. A Set PA is involved in the shoot on the set, and so is often considered slightly higher in status than an Office PA. Any time a PA is assigned to interact with the talent (not extras a.k.a. background) that is a slightly higher status job.

But other than that, PAs are there to do all kinds of jobs from fetching and carrying, "locking up" (making sure everyone knows that the camera is rolling, so there is silence when the

27

scenes are being shot), distributing sides (script pages of just that day's work in half size), watching out for people wandering on to the set, cleaning up messes, and sometimes helping out various departments with non-specialized tasks. A PA might be tapped by the Grip Department to hold a flag, or by the Art Department On-set Dresser to help move some furniture. One way you can tell a very low budget picture is if a PA has been assigned to run Craft Service (the on-set refreshments table), instead of hiring a professional for that position. You'd think there would be no difference - it's just snacks, right? But oh-my-goodness, there is. Good Craft Service professionals take just as much pride in doing a fantastic job as any other skilled pro on a movie set, or anywhere else.

PAs are generalists, but in terms of your film career, it is not good to be seen as such. Film production companies are made up of people who are specialists in their jobs. The higher the budget the more you can hire specialists. Note that when a Director does more than one thing, they get more than one credit. The goal of any PA is to never be a PA again.

The Right Format

The most important section of any production resume is your credits - the past films or TV projects on which you worked. Remember:

The fact that your resumes are based on Credits, rather than past Jobs and Duties, is the primary difference between a production crew resume and a resume for any other kind of job.

Sometimes this can be problematic when all you have done is student films. But if those are your only credits, so be it. One of main the purposes of interning is so that you might have some more pro credits to add to your resume - the other two purposes being starting your networking, and learning how things are done.

As far as student film credits go, many people want to show the breadth of their experience, all their technical accomplishments - especially if they feel like they were a successful one-man band. However, that can make for a pretty messy resume. No real production hires an entry level person to be their DP or even their focus puller (1st A.C.) - although a Camera Department PA might be in the cards. Choose one or at most two positions from each project to use on your credit list. In a moment, you will see a way to write out your credits that will help keep it all neat.

Credits should be organized by *type of project*. That is the way it is done on **IMDbPro** (as distinct from the public version of IMDb.) Doing them this way allows you to customize your resume to different gigs. For example, for a TV application, move the whole TV section to the top.

The usual sections are: Feature Films, Cable/TV, Shorts, Documentary, Industrials, Commercials, Student films. There are also Web Series, although there is some debate about whether these should have their own category or be under TV. I tend towards the latter along with Cable and streaming services.

Eventually you would leave student films off altogether, unless they happened to be an award winner of some kind or were accepted into a film festival. Note: that is everyone's student films, not just your own directorial efforts. Also, a UCLA Thesis counts as student, until someone buys it for distribution.

Within each section, most of the time you would organize your credits chronologically, by year of release. Sometimes it helps to put an especially notable production at the top.

When you are working in a specific department, I like to put that department head on the credit, along with the producer. The purpose is to highlight the members of your network – people who work in the same department often know each other.

This is what your credits should look like, from my resume: From this image, you will see a couple of technical formatting points:

*Write the title of the film or show in *italics*.

*In brackets, put the year the film was released or the program was broadcast - *not* the dates that you worked. Some projects take years to gain distribution and release. I worked on *Seventh Veil* (2003) in early 1999.

*Add the production company/ies or the Network.

*Name the Producer and Director.

*You can name your Department Head.

*Write your job title, which would be your credit on the project. Make it bold and it will stand out visually.

Credits - Feature Films

Seventh Veil (2003)	Heron International Pictures Director: Armin Q. Chaudri	**Production Designer**
Special Delivery (1999)	The Calling LLC Prod: Marci & Scott Wellman Prod Design: William V. Ryder	**Art Director**
True Friends (1998)	2nd Generation Films Prod/Dir: James Quattrochi * *Winner Gold Medal – North Carolina Film Festival, 1998*	**Production Designer**
Love Kills (1998)	Love Kills LLC Prod/Dir: Mario Van Peebles Prod Design: W. Brooke Wheeler	**Set Decorator**
The Nurse (1997)	Trimark/IV Productions/Image Prod: Richard Brandes, Pierre David; Dir: Rob Malenfant	**Production Designer**
Man of Her Dreams (1997)	Image Organization/Live Prod: Pierre David, Ken Sanders; Dir: Marty Kitrosser	**Production Designer**
Motel Blue (1997)	Blproductions, Inc Prod: Steven J. Anderson Prod Design: W. Brooke Wheeler	**Set Decorator**
Kid Cop (1996)	Brainstorm Media Prod: Meyer Shwarzstein, Noel Zanitsch	**Production Designer**
The Dentist (1996)	Trimark/HBO Prod: Pierre David Prod Design: William V. Ryder	**Art Director/Set Decorator**

After the Director or Department Head, it is nice to add the stars, if they are at all notable. This is another way to clarify the budget level of the film. You will also notice that I noted an award that one of my films won at a festival.

For your student films - which will be their own category - where you Produced, Directed and did some other thing (often Writer), you could put your name in the "Prod/Dir" slot and then add the other thing in the job title spot. Or separate "Producer" under the company name, and use "Director" as the job title. Don't do a whole ton of hyphenates. As a student film, it is rather expected that you most likely also Edited, maybe operated the Camera and managed the locations.

What is *not* included in the Credits list are the duties of each position on any movie. The UPM or other Department Head who will interview you already knows the duties. It is an error to attempt to show off what you know, especially at entry-level, rather than simply state what you have done. At entry-level, and even beyond, everyone knows more than you, no matter how many student projects you have completed.

Also, there is no need to include details about the film's format or run time, and certainly do not include the log line or synopsis.

Eventually, you will be a specialist and your resume will include everything except the individual job titles, because your job title will be in the letterhead. It will look more like this one, my husband's. Note the film titles bolded, but still in italics.

James H. Coburn IV, C.A.S.   Production Sound Mixer   310.413.XXXX

FEATURE FILMS

The Bronx Bull
(2014)

Sunset Pictures/That's Hollywood
Dir: Martin Guigui; Prod: Ron Singer, Scott Reed
With William Forsythe, Joe Mantegna, Paul Sorvino, Natasha Henstridge &
Penelope Ann Miller

All's Faire in Love
(2009)

That's Hollywood/Patriot Pictures/Duke of York/Gold Rush Pictures
Dir: Scott Marshall; Prod: Ron Singer, Scott Reed
With Christina Ricci, Owen Benjamin, Matthew Lilliard & Ann-Margret

Hit and Run
(2009)

Ithaka Entertainment/That's Hollywood/Metro-Goldwyn-Mayer/Maverick Films
Dir: Enda McCallion; Prod: Brent Emory, Mark Morgan, Braxton Pope, Andrew Weiner
With Laura Breckenridge, Kevin Corrigan & Christopher Shand

The Strange Case of
Dr. Jekyll & Mr. Hyde
(2006)

Fantastical Cinema LLC/Motion Picture Corporation
Dir: John Carl Buecher; Prod: Peter Davy
With Tony Todd, Tracy Scoggins

From Mexico with Love Cinamour/BDS Productions
(2009)

Dir: Jimmy Nickerson; Prod: Glen Hartford, Daniel Toll
With Bruce McGill, Steven Bauer & Kuno Becker

Forbidden Warrior-
The Prequel (2005)

Cinamour/BDS Productions/That's Hollywood/Samurai Prods. Inc
Dir: Jimmy Nickerson; Prod: Glen Hartford, Daniel Toll
With Marie Matiko, Sung Kang, Karl Yune & Tony Amendola

Landspeed
(2002)

Landspeed Productions LLC/Unified Film Organization/City Heat Productions
Dir: Christian McIntire; Prod: Jeffery Beach, Ken Oldandt, Phillip J. Roth
With Billy Zane, Ray Wise & Pamela Gidley

Beneath Loch Ness
(2001)

Loch Ness Productions/Brimstone Ent LLC/Dimension Films
Dir: Chuck Comisky; Prod: Scott Vandiver
With Lysette Anthony, Patrick Bergin & Brian Wimmer

Cahoots
(2001)

Chewing School/Den Pictures Inc
Dir: Dirk Benedict; Prod: John Stronach, Mike Erwin, J. Max Kirishima
With Keith Carradine, David Keith & Janet Gunn11

Credits for the body of an Email

Every now and then, a hirer will specify that your resume
should be in the body of the email message rather than an
attachment. This could trash your pretty formatting across the

page. Therefore, have your credits in a document that you can copy and paste into the body of an e-mail if asked for it. Use a brief version of your cover letter as the intro. **Justify to the left** like this:

Film Title (YEAR)
Production Company
Producer
Director
With stars if well-known
Your Job Title

CHAPTER 5: OTHER WORK EXPERIENCE

When you are just starting out, with few credits, your other jobs will assume a greater importance. You want to show the transferable skills, and outstanding personal qualities that will make you an asset to any production, even though superficially there appears to be nothing remotely similar between your summer gig at a fast food restaurant and working as PA for a post-production facility.

Put your other jobs after your Credits and Skills sections. Eventually you will have sufficient credits that these outside industry jobs will drop off your resume as irrelevant.

To save time with later customizing, it is probably simplest to just go ahead and format your work experience on any resume as if for an ATS. Personally, I hate that ATS need to see the dates of your employment after the employer and the job title. It seems completely backwards to me, visually and intuitively. But I don't write the algorithms. I have changed my own policy with my clients, and now format the Work Experience sections of all resumes to ATS guidelines, just to keep it simple for updating. See more in **Chapter 14: ATS vs Human**.

If you want to format your work experience in what is more appealing manner for human consumption, then I applaud your enthusiasm - but do be sure to have a second ATS optimized version standing by. Remember, people working in freelance fields must update their resume a lot more often - in the case of film production, after every gig.

The ATS standard way of writing out "Work Experience" is:

Employer, City, ST   Job Title   Month/year - Month/year

Then bullet point your job duties, incorporating descriptors.

I like to make it more readable for humans like this:

EMPLOYER, City, ST   **Job Title**   Mon/year - Mon/year

The dates should be justified to the right-side margin. I'm told that you can write them either as 01/2016 or Jan 2016. Remember: Tabs or spaces, not Columns.

Tip: Start keeping a record of your start and finish dates for every job now. In 5 years you might need that information.

Highlight Relevant Duties

Duties should always be bulleted. It is nice to layer bullets. Often if you feel the urge to write "and…" that is a sign that you may need another bullet. Remember, you need not stick to one page, so it is alright to take up some space.

On the other hand, brevity in expression is highly desirable. Think about the kind of qualities that a PA must possess - ability to listen to instructions, tenacity in follow through, ability to focus and strong attention to detail, energy and discipline, observant, cheerful, willing to do anything needed and get one's hands dirty, quick thinking, team player, courteous and discreet, aware of deadlines and timeliness, a safe driver. Concisely stress any job duties that highlight those characteristics. If the duties are truly not transferable, it is better to stick to a single bullet.

Pay less attention to the job duties that are about other qualities - leadership or supervisory skills, sales skills, writing skills, coding, social media communication (except Office PA), equipment operation, creativity (seriously - they don't want someone who always has an opinion at this level). It is not that you don't have those abilities - just that they are not generally relevant to an entry level PA gig.

Other Employment

MALIBU CAFE, Malibu, CA   **Server**   Aug 2014 – Aug 2015
- Offered superb guest service in popular casual eatery
- Collected guest orders, ran food to tables, helped bus tables; POS system & cash handling
- Provided guests with information about the local area

JAMBA JUICE, Malibu, CA   **Team Member**   April 2013 – Aug 2014
- Offered excellent customer service and order prep, maintaining consistent high standards of national refreshment chain
- Greeted guests; used POS system/cashier
- Clean up duties

Incorporating your references into your experience

Sometimes it can be helpful to incorporate your references into the past job item. This is especially helpful when you have few credits or past jobs, to help lengthen the resume appropriately.

Use a bullet to indicate the name and job title of your supervisor, and their phone number. Maybe italicize or bold the name to help it stand out visually.

RRRR Advertising Group, Zelienople, PA   **Advertising Intern** May-Aug 2012
- Strong multitasking - market research, heavy phones, filing and office duties
- Company BASE strategy, content rippling and data entry with strong attention to detail
- Supervisor: Brianna Smith, Creative Strategist 724.xxx.xxxx

State College Hockey, State College, PA   **Marketing Intern** Jul 2011–May 2012
- Program design for events using MS Word templates requiring focus and eye for detail
- Photography and image manipulation using Photoshop
- Supervisor: John Brown, VP Hockey & Business Admin. 716.xxx.xxxx

---

A special note to Veterans

Many people coming out of film school are military veterans. I have noticed that many of you tend to either forget that your military duties and specialties contain many excellent transferable skills and don't write your service down as a job, or to forget that we civilians are ignorant of the practical meanings behind some of the descriptive jargon.

With my veteran clients, I always encourage them to drill down to the actual day-to-day activities behind the duty designations. It is the details of what a "Logistics Specialist" did each day, and the skills entailed in that job, that help you get your first gigs in film production. On the next page is an example.

These duties could be improved by some added

descriptions such as "with strong attention to detail", "using strong verbal communication" or "requiring consistent multi-tasking", as well as some added metrics such as the frequency of missions and reports ("daily", "weekly"). If I were composing this today, I would also re-order the dates, employer and job titles.

2008-2011   **Supply Supervisor** (Logistical Field), US Army - Soto Cano, Honduras; Fort Sill, OK
Rank: Supply Sergeant; Hazardous Materials Compliance Certificate; Field Sanitation Certificate; Warrior Leadership Course
Supervised supply & arms room; trained personnel; coordinated all supply activities and records; purchasing; maintained inventory control of equipment worth $6.2Million.

2003-2006   **Supply Specialist**, US Army – Fort Lee, VA; Fort Sill, OK;
Operation Iraqi Freedom, Iraq
Unit Supply Specialist Diploma
Ensured combat unit had all needed gear, food & utilities to complete missions; maintained sensitive item reports; managed logistics & records; liaised with civilian contractors

---

No Experience Whatsoever

What if you have none, truly zero work experience outside of your studies?

This is what internships are for. My strongest advice is to you is not to squander your time in college, but to make a friend of the internship coordinator.

Don't neglect your networking and don't be too proud to take advantage of nepotism. I was lucky. When I was in high school, my mother's old friend and colleague gave me my first job in show business, as a favor to her - and I turned out to be good enough at it to be hired again. At the end of high school, two years later, I had saved enough money to buy my first car. Who do you know? Who do your parents know?

CHAPTER 6: EDUCATION SECTION

For production resumes, I generally put the Education section last. Your credits and work experience are usually more important to Producers than your studies.

For your Education, you need only to note your highest qualification, unless there is something very extraordinary about your earlier achievements. Do not put your high school once you have graduated college. You probably don't need your BA if you have an MA or MFA, unless they are in divergent fields and you think it will be helpful. Someone who has a Fine Arts degree and an MBA would want to note both - perfect qualifications for a Producer!

Historically, one would write the degree or qualification first, the year of graduation, followed by the university. Like all the other ATS specific formatting, it feels backwards compared to tradition, but for those resumes, your education should be written out like this:

School, City, State - **Degree** (any specialty), YEAR
- Any special awards
- Maybe GPA, if it is very high for ATS resumes. Do include it if specifically required in the job listing

The year is the year you graduated from college. I have

seen people indicate (year - year) all the time they were at school, and there is some debate as to the correctness of this regarding ATS resumes. However, the experts at the University of Chicago recommend only using the "date - date" information when you have incomplete degrees, are now out of school, but spent some time studying. Start with your most recent degree or course of study.

Here is how I write out mine across the page:

University of Wollongong, Wollongong, AUSTRALIA - **Bachelor of Creative Arts (Hons) -** Theatre Design and Technology, 1990

You could also write it on two lines:

University of Wollongong, Wollongong, AUSTRALIA

- Bachelor of Creative Arts (Hons) - Theatre Design and Technology, 1990

I write out the whole degree for clarity, since I am from another country, and the letters "BCA" might not make sense to many people in the US, but most of the time it is reasonable to write the abbreviation. I like to write the institution in italics, just to create visual variety and make it stand out.

What if you are still in college? It is correct to write your degree out this way:

School, City, ST - **Degree** and specialty (Expected Month, YEAR)

42

Then once you finish, you can alter "Expected" to the year of graduation.

If you have Professional Development qualifications - courses studied while employed - those should also go in the Education section. This is a good place to note things like Avid Certifications.

Grammar note for writing about your degrees: You *are* a Bachelor or Associate or Master of Arts or Science etc. You *have* a degree with the shorthand being Bachelor's, Associate's or Master's degree. The shorthand is *possessive, not plural.* So please put in *the apostrophe.*

So, what about film school? Is it worth it?

When I first started in film after many years in theater, I was fortunate to be trained by some people already working. I got to see how an art department worked, the difference between theater and film scenic painting, and particularly to be shown the ropes in on-set dressing by a good one. In a way, I was an apprentice for a short time. I found I had an affinity for the work. This is where internships – with real productions – are useful.

However, it is crucial to learn from people who are working properly. I can't count the number of community level theaters I have been part of where the stage managers don't know how to make up The Book or mark up a rehearsal space, or where they don't know the proper way to manage a tech week. It can be frustrating to work with amateurs, and it is a shame to see new people muddled by learning the wrong way (wrong in comparison to commercial, professional theater) to do things.

Even when I was working on a couple of films shot in regional centers, some of the others with plenty of Hollywood experience would say, "This isn't a real movie", although they couldn't explain exactly why. I didn't know the difference then, but it had to do with budget and the compromises made to manage with low budgets.

Know your purpose in attending film school

Film, and for that matter theater, are two industries where professional success is possible in the absence of a degree. As time goes on, perhaps it is more difficult to rise to the very top of the business, such as a Studio chief, without one, but a decent living coming up "through the ranks" is perfectly possible - with hard work and a lot of networking.

Therefore, it is good to know your reasons for attending film school and starting your professional life with the debt these studies will likely incur.

Here are some valuable gains from attending college for film:

Access to equipment and facilities– at film school you should have access and opportunity to use higher quality – i.e. more expensive – equipment for your own projects, and the opportunity to work in professional level facilities including sound stages and editing suites. Always think ahead to your reel.

Community of colleagues– most of the time you will be studying with the same group of people for anything from 2-4 years. You will form friendships and have the chance to appreciate many different artistic visions. These people are your first network.

Opportunity to create your own projects– especially risky projects. The facilities and resources of your school allow you to be experimental in relative safety.

Starting your design/craft portfolio. Take lots of pictures!

Feedback– you will have the opportunity to receive feedback without the serious consequences of the real world – being fired, or gaining a reputation for problems, or losing a bunch of money.

Access to internships with higher end companies. Many of the best internship opportunities are reserved for officially enrolled students. Some specify recent graduates.

Instruction– a well-organized curriculum and thoughtful instructors will direct your attention towards the specific skills you will need to realize your vision and craft a long-term career. You can learn the right or best procedures.

I'm very glad that I attended college. Having a degree of any kind can be helpful for securing certain kinds of employment, including in show business. However, nobody ever asked me for my transcript or cared about my grades. Film and theater jobs, I got from referrals and recommendations. They didn't want to know the details of my degree, just that I was qualified. Other employers who were interested in the mere existence of my degree were retail stores, offices (including at studios) and academic institutions. In my experience, the only people who care about actual grades are admissions officers for higher degree studies.

What attaining a degree from a film or theater school shows prospective employers is *your seriousness* and *commitment to the industry*. It shows that you can complete a long-term project; that is, it shows your tenacity.

A film school degree is not the only useful path to success in the film biz. Aspiring producers and studio heads might choose a business degree or even a law degree, while screenwriters might seek out a creative writing program rather than a film school.

If you are going to attend college I urge you to throw yourself into as many projects as you can and keep a seeking attitude foremost in your mind. And make a friend of the internship coordinator.

CHAPTER 7: CUSTOMIZING YOUR RESUME

Why do this?

The number one complaint of HR people, and other hirers too, is that most of the resumes they receive are not customized, feel like form letters, or don't properly highlight the relevant experience by being a kitchen sink of "one-size-fits-none" generalities. It hurts people's feelings when they think you don't consider their job important enough to customize for. But more than that, it hurts your job prospects.

Some people think customizing applies only to cover letters. Yes, you absolutely must customize your cover letter, but you should go further and customize your resume too.

It is not enough to merely make one resume for PA jobs and one for waiting tables - although even that is a start that many naive job seekers fail to make. You must customize your resume to every job application. Every time.

So, customize. Not just the ATS applications either. All of them. It might be something as simple as moving a credit section or highlighting a couple of credits where you already worked with someone on the crew list. It might mean tweaking the language of your skills to being more formal or less so, based on what you can learn about the company or the UPM. It might be as small as reordering your skills to bring one set to the top.

Or it might be that there are no changes needed other than the salutation on the cover email.

But take the time to read over the documents before you send them and look for any opportunities to tweak them to the job or company.

When you are handing a DS resume to a contact, you exchange the keyword information that you would glean from a listing, for the infinitely more valuable personal referral. However, sometimes it is possible to learn enough about a production company or the stakeholders involved to make a reasonable guess as to the kind of language that will garner a more favorable response, even in one of these resumes.

Research the Company and the People

Read all you can about the company, including developing a familiarity with their past products. The company website will contain the kind of language that reflects their company culture. Look up the principal individuals on IMDb and their social media profiles. Learn something about their history. Check out their YouTube accounts.

From IMDb continue to examine linked projects. Notice whether they have long term relationships with crew members with repeat hires, and what kind of projects the crew members moved on to. Did they all evidently leave the industry never to be heard from again? That could be a red flag.

I always like to input people's names into the Book search on Google. This will find if someone has been referred to in the content of an increasing-by-the-day number of published works including some magazines. It can be fun to do that.

If you are sending a resume based on your networking (which should be most of the time) what can you glean from your last encounter with the hirer? Where was the event? Were they enjoying it, or was it an obligation? What was your conversation about? Was the person lively, articulate, a film buff and seemed creative, or were they businesslike, straightforward and focused on the business aspects of the industry? Many people are all these things, but not necessarily all at the same time.

Remember, they are doing you a favor by looking at your resume. Make them glad they did by showing them how you could be helpful and useful to them, rather than focusing on what you hope to gain from them.

Addressing your resume

Hopefully you have been invited to send your resume and will address it to the person you know. If you are sending your resume cold (see the upcoming chapter on Cold Calling), it is still a good thing to find out the name of the UPM or Department Head on the project. Finding out that name is the most basic research you can do.

Visual Appeal

It is a shame that most ATS go into a tizzy with most of the techniques that people use to make their resume appealing, like boxes, lines across the page or shading. If you are doing a DS resume, why not make it pleasant to look at? Shading certainly makes the headings stand out. For some creative jobs, even color can look appealing. But don't overdo it.

Here's how shading looks on *my* resume.

Feature Films

Seventh Veil (2003)	Heron International Pictures Director: Armin Q. Chaudri	**Production Designer**
Special Delivery (1999)	The Calling LLC Prod: Marci & Scott Wellman; Prod Design: William V. Ryder	**Art Director**
True Friends (1998)	2nd Generation Films Prod/Dir: James Quattrochi	**Production Designer**

* Winner Gold Medal – North Carolina Film Festival, 1998

Vince & The Trailer Park (1998)	BSA Productions Prod: Bryan Lorenz	**Production Coordinator**
Love Kills (1998)	Love Kills LLC Prod/Dir: Mario Van Peebles; Prod Design: W. Brooke Wheeler	**Set Decorator**
The Nurse (1997)	Trimark/IV Productions/Image Prod: Richard Brandes, Pierre David; Dir: Rob Malenfant	**Production Designer**
Man of Her Dreams (1997)	Image Organization/Live Prod: Pierre David, Ken Sanders; Dir: Marty Kitrosser	**Production Designer**
Motel Blue (1997)	Blproductions, Inc Prod: Steven J. Anderson; Prod Design: W. Brooke Wheeler	**Set Decorator**
Kid Cop (1996)	Brainstorm Media Prod: Meyer Shwarzstein, Noel Zanitsch	**Production Designer**
The Dentist (1996)	Trimark/HBO Prod: Pierre David; Prod Design: William V. Ryder	**Art Director/Set Decorator**
Club VR & Deadly Charades (1996)	Mystique Films Prod Design: Jesse Johnston	**Set Decorator**
One Man's Justice (1996) Aka *One Tough Bastard*	LIVE Entertainment Prod Design: Terri Schaetzle	**On-Set Dresser**
Serial Killer (1995)	Inferno Productions Dir: Pierre David; Prod Design: W. Brooke Wheeler	**On-Set Dresser**
Cage II (1994)	Rocket Pictures Prod Design: William V. Ryder	**On-Set Dresser/Scenic**
Love and a .45 (1994)	Trimark Dir: C.M. Talkington	**Scenic painter/2nd Unit** **Art Dept. Coordinator**

Television

Yesterday's Target (1996)	Showtime/IRS Media Prod: Albert T. Dickerson, Larry Estes Prod Design: William V. Ryder	**Art Director**
The Secretary (1995)	CBS/Agenda Productions Prod: Pierre David; Prod Design: William V. Ryder	**On-Set Dresser**

CHAPTER 8: FINDING YOUR JOB LEADS

Job Hunting

If you are not employed, you should consider finding work your full-time job. You should spend close to 40 hours a week in job search related activities. You will see that not all of these are in the 9-5 business hours, just like film work! These include:

- Network!
  - o Go to industry networking events
  - o Organize and manage your calendar - keep records of your expenses for your tax return
  - o Call or email your colleagues and past work buddies just to keep in touch
  - o Contribute to discussions on relevant networking groups, and comment on blog posts, such as those on LinkedIn, Facebook, Stage 32, ProductionHUB, or other individuals' blogs
- Keep your resume up to date and updated on all your online sites
  - o Update your online portfolio, if relevant
- Edit/update your reel and post it
- Send applications to relevant jobs from job boards and listings
  - o Research the companies that are hiring, and the individuals that work there

- o   Customize your resume and cover letter to these listings
- Cold call productions from production listings
- Follow up on sent resumes
- Read the trades and keep abreast of current and new trends in the business
- Practice your interview skills and answers to likely questions
- Prep your personal presentation for interviews

Other useful ways to spend your work time between gigs include:
- Keep up with your writing and project development ideas
  - o   Meet with your creative writers' support group, or other peer support group
- Professional development
  - o   Take classes related to your craft
  - o   Read, and/or watch videos about it
- Read scripts, including classic ones
- Read biographies of people you admire and hope to emulate
- Study the history of film and television (yes, really!!)
- Make short films, including with your smart phone
- Volunteer with an industry organization or local film festival - although be aware that this might require a commitment that could prevent you being available for a gig
- Watch movies and TV shows - with a critical eye
  - o   Do this last! Don't use this activity as an excuse to

procrastinate the more prosaic but essential tasks

o Write film reviews and critiques on your blog or other sites

When you are on a job - a movie or TV show - or have a day job, many of these activities move to your leisure time. But it is crucial to keep your resume updated and that you look for your next gig while you are still in your current one. Make calls on your own time - your lunch break and before work. It is great to be able to say, "I'm working as a Set PA on *THIS MOVIE*, but we wrap on thus-and-such date" or "I'm working in post right now on *THIS MOVIE*, but I'll be available in three weeks."

Recently there has been a proliferation of online social networking and professional networking sites, including some specific to the film industry. You should upload your best resume (and update it as needed) to LinkedIn, Pinterest, Google +, Below the Line's site, and your professional Facebook page (as distinct from personal profile). You can consider the new industry social media sites Stage 32, Variety 411, and ProductionHUB, depending on your willingness and ability to pay a monthly fee.

Tag your resume posts with the proper keyword tags to aid the search engines. These include words like your job title, the department you work in, "film", "movies", "television", genres like "Reality TV" or "Comedy series", and "crew". If you have some special characteristics or skills add them to the tags, E.G. "Avid certified", "Movie Magic expert".

LinkedIn is used as a search engine by recruiters, and tags are vital. Did you know that Pinterest is a huge search engine too? It isn't just about people collecting pretty pictures like a digital mood board any more. People pin full articles and videos. Book authors get enormous amounts of business via their Pinned promo blog posts. You can use Pinterest boards to help direct people to your own website, LinkedIn profile or YouTube Channel for your reel and ongoing work.

All the advice about social media marketing of one's business applies to entertainment industry job hunters too. To raise your profile in the business, contribute - make thoughtful comments on blog posts or posted articles, reply to questions, and share information. Don't just ask for job leads or support for your projects. Be an ongoing presence, rather than someone who only posts when they have something to announce. You never know when you might meet someone in person who liked something you said on line. In disagreement, be courteous. Probably avoid political discussions which often turn heated. Don't burn your bridges before you have even crossed them.

Production Listings and Job Boards

About any paid membership service, *Caveat Emptor*. The internet has created a proliferation of sites claiming to have unique access to jobs, people and companies. Often it turns out that the jobs are not exclusive after all. Some sites are like Trivago - their bots collect listings from other places and stack them onto a page, so they can be very efficient, but hardly exclusive. Others display the jobs but only allow access to the contact information to paid members in a tiered system. Others claim to curate jobs for you specifically for your resume, or submit your resume to relevant employer posters, again in a tiered manner depending on your subscription. The problem with this is obviously that you have not been able to fine tune your customization. Higher end companies often specify no "agency" submissions.

Some services will send you a nice email when a job with your keywords comes up, which is designed to save time. My experience with those is that the duties or qualifications of the listing are often only tangentially related to the job titles and I always wonder whether I'm missing out on listings, so they don't make me feel confident or secure. I prefer to be more proactive and search the job listing sites regularly. (I'm not searching for me but keeping my eyes open on behalf of my clients.)

These services are usually free to employers, as compared to a newspaper which charges people per line to post a positions vacant listing. As a result, one thing I have noticed is that most of the crew jobs listed on these services are very low budget - seeking interns or free labor, or very low paying. In other words, the hirers are often people who are early in their own careers with shallow networks. Despite the glowing testimonials quoted on the home pages, I have not yet been told of successes in using these sites by any of my own clients. Your mileage may vary.

Here's a secret: Real, properly budgeted movies rarely need to advertise for crew because they fill most of their Heads of Department from the Producer's rolodex, and most of the rest of the crew via referrals. The exception is when a picture or show is going to a regional center, and they need local crew. Of course, the first place they will look is the regional Film Commission's crew roster, so if you live and want to work anywhere other than Los Angeles or New York, **make sure you connect with your local Film Commission.**

I strongly advise everyone who asks, to subscribe to **Below the Line Production Listings,** http://www.findfilmwork.com/, especially once they come to Los Angeles. It is a paid service, but reasonably and fairly priced in comparison to others. You may also want to subscribe to their free newsletter which has a ton of great articles, video content and interviews. It is a way to stay current on upcoming events and even find some networking events to attend. The listings include local, regional and international shoots. There are other production listing services, but BTL is the best, in my opinion. (Again, YMMV.)

BTL listings are sourced actively by their researchers who contact production companies for updates, and so are very comprehensive and generally accurate. Since they are updated daily, there are fewer instances of a film having already shot being listed as "In Production", and they have several development categories. You can take advantage of the features that BTL provides, like making notes via your profile of your past searches, which projects you contacted when and other pertinent and helpful info right in the individual listings. They often name a vast number of the people working on the project - which they have space for since it is online, as compared to something analog, like The Hollywood Reporter's printed production listings back in the olden days.

Once upon a time, THR and Daily Variety's listings, which came out on two different weekdays, were the only way to find out about upcoming productions (other than your networking sources of course!). Back then, it was possible to subscribe to just that day's paper, rather than the full weekly subscription, but it still wasn't cheap. Other services snail-mailed production listings to their subscribers, and later turned to much faster e-mail communiques. Thank goodness times have changed, because online listings seem to stay far more updated, which means less chance of missing out during the hiring phase.

Every now and then you will find an error on BTL, or a project that has collapsed, changed producers, or moved out of town, but most of the time if they say they are "In Preparation", they *are* in Prep. If they say "Pre-Production", they haven't started

Principle Photography yet. By having lots of names attached to each project, you can see if there is anyone you know working on it.

I also recommend **Entertainment Careers dot net.** http://www.entertainmentcareers.net/ I have seen many of the same jobs advertised on paid subscription job services that appear on EC for free to view, usually including the contact information. It is an exception to my usual warning about free services. That being said, the membership may be worth buying for some. Membership allows access to even more jobs, especially some of the higher end internships, as well as facilitating online applications. There tend to be quite a few TV positions advertised on EC, and periodically studio support jobs, rather than actual crew gigs. You can subscribe to a weekly update of new jobs, and search the job listings by numerous filters, including by State, and categories, including job functions. It is possible to drill down to three or four jobs on which to concentrate your applications, per search.

Another great use for Entertainment Careers is as a career planning resource. Start at the top job to which you aspire - you will learn the kind of qualifications needed, and duties that this person undertakes. Then usually towards the bottom of the page, there will be the expected degree, and the experience required - some number of years in a related position or subordinate one. You can follow the "positions ladder" down and see the career paths that someone at the top would likely have followed, and how long it took them. It may give you ideas about your own qualifications and where you might need to upgrade your skills.

You can still look for work in the business through traditional sources - the trades, industry journals that have classifieds sections, and the daily papers' employment columns. You are unlikely to find actual crew work in there, but you may find related jobs advertised like support positions at Studios or production companies. These are the kind of gigs for which you should use your ATS optimized resume.

The other places to examine for job listings include the Studios' and Networks' own sites, and the Careers pages of major production and post-production companies' sites. Much of the time, these jobs do turn up on EntertainmentCareers.net within a few days of posting, but not always.

Network, network, network

A networking event is any time people from the film business get together for any reason at all.

Examples include:

- Visiting the set when someone you know is working (by invitation)
- Wrap parties
- Crew screenings

- Industry screenings (especially often during Awards season)
- Parties connected with any of the Awards
- Vendor events like informational sessions about new products
- Industry Association mixers or events/educational seminars
- Industry Expos like the Locations Expo
- The rental counter at an industry vendor
- Film festival screenings and connected events. Concentrate on professional ones, rather than those aimed at the general public
- Other cultural or community activities, like your church, when you learn that some of your community are in the business

Less helpful are those nutty notions like frequenting the bars or restaurants (or AA meetings) where industry folk hang out - unless you are joining your working-in-the-biz-friend who is with a group of colleagues at the said bar.

Have your **elevator pitch** ready. This often refers to writers telling people about the script they just finished, but in your case, this is less than 10 seconds about your job search when the other person asks about you. Hopefully you already have their name and have asked them who they are. Practice saying your pitch aloud so that it comes out smoothly and sounds natural.

Here are some examples of elevator pitches from my clients:

- I've been working at an animal shelter while I studied film makeup. I recently graduated, and although I eventually want to work in Special Effects makeup, for right now I want to get started as a PA and learn more about film.
- I just moved to town from Austin, TX. I worked a couple of local features there and had my own digital content production company. Now I'm looking for work in production.
- I've been working in talent booking and casting for talk shows and conventions back East, but my dream is to be a Show Runner and producer. I'm looking for work as an Assistant while I'm developing a documentary about health and fitness.
- I just got back from a fantastic summer internship at a Film Festival in London, where I got to edit some promo videos. Now I'm back in school and looking for my next internship, which I hope will be in post-production.
- Since I moved here from Ohio, I've been working as a PA on commercials, but my dream is to be an Editor. I'm looking for a Post PA or Assistant Editor gig.

No time wasted! Then **pause** to let them ask you about SOMETHING you mentioned. Hopefully they will do so. Then when you can, ask a question about the other person - *not* "do you know of any jobs". Even "what about you?" is good enough.

This is **relationship building time**. As you continue to talk you will have the chance to mention the other interesting things you have done. Chances are the other person will know of something coming up, or someone who is hiring, or a new project about to happen. Give out your business card and collect theirs. That is the purpose of a card, by the way, to collect their card in exchange.

These short pitches show several things about you:

- You are committed and ambitious enough to take the risk of coming out here.
- You know the lingo.
- Your immediate background - you may have studied, or you have some related experience.
- You are humble, with reasonable expectations of entry level work.

The other person may be looking for people to work for free on nonsense. They might be quick to make offers to you and talk up their thesis project and talk about credits for your resume. Suddenly they are the supplicant. I would say polite things like "it sounds like an interesting project. I'll think about it, but I really need to find paid work as soon as I can. Can I take your card?"

Exceptions –

- Someone who has access to a proper internship program through a big production company or studio. Go to any interview that gets you on to a Lot.
- Someone who has a surprisingly big-name star on their low budget show. This is often the sign of a second-generation person, or someone changing gigs (EG. a designer directing for the first time) who is calling in some favors, so the network is of a higher level than the budget might suggest.
- Your already-close-friend's project.

Follow up with an e-mail to the people looking for free labor, (thanks, sorry I can't help you this time) and a phone call to the real prospects or friends.

You will notice that your elevator pitch includes nothing about wanting to direct one day. That is because all that will do is make you disappear into the crowd of wannabes. EVERYONE in this town wants to direct, or write and direct, one day. That is why "but I really want to direct" is a punch line. If you have something unusual about yourself or your work, that will make you memorable, that is something to include in your elevator pitch.

Eventually people will ask you about your ambitions, or even if you want to direct. Then you can tell them about it.

LinkedIn, Social Media and your website

I've already mentioned in passing that you should spend time updating your LinkedIn site - this simply means adding each new job as you get them and making sure that any resume linked is also most current.

It is also a good idea to have a social media presence, and maybe your own website if you like to write. There are apps that will automatically link your blog posts to your Facebook page and Twitter. You should always announce when you are about to start a project, and when it is about to wrap, keeping it upbeat of course. It should go without saying - don't use your blog as a forum for dissing the production or complaining about your colleagues or bosses. There is an old saw: You meet the same people on your down that you met on your way up. Be memorable for your good work, energy and kindness.

My clients will often use the Summary section from their ATS style resume for their LinkedIn profile summary. Then they can generally copy and paste the job duties from each job, using as wide a range of synonyms as possible. These are the keywords that are used by search engines.

People in show business tend to use "Freelance {Job Title}

in Film/Television" or something similar on their LinkedIn list of jobs to cover a long time span of numerous projects. This is OK if you are very busy and have a strong network of production contacts. However, if you are looking for a Studio, Network or production company staff job, you could optimize your keywords by taking the time to write out each of your credits as if they were employers. The same tactic is useful for people new to the business or recent grads with few jobs in their history.

When using credits as if they were employers for LinkedIn, it is useful for SEO to include job duties. (I already mentioned that these are not usually included on credits on production resumes because the UPM/Line Producer already knows what every job on the film set entails.) Remember, you can make each entry visually appealing and organized by using bullets.

Like ATS, LinkedIn likes metrics. If you know the budget of your film, or your department, you can insert that information into the item. If you supervised a team, include the number of people. If you worked on a series, note the number of episodes or hours of content.

People who are just there on the social media sites with terrific resumes but not making actual applications, are what recruiters call "passive candidates". Remember that LinkedIn is a resource for HR people, recruiters and headhunters, who treat it as a search engine. They have a specific list of skills and responsibilities (i.e. keywords) that they seek to match. They may not have the insider knowledge that a Producer has about the business. A Producer can tell at a glance what budget level you have been working at just from the familiar film titles and the other names in the credits. HR people need to be told.

Join some of the relevant groups on LinkedIn, such as *Film & TV Professionals*, and contribute to discussions. This only touches on the ever-increasing features available on LinkedIn, such as SlideShare (http://www.slideshare.net) where in addition to graphic presentations, you can also embed You Tube videos. You could create a slide show of your portfolio and embed your reel.

The Low Budget World

The kinds of leads that you find in free sources, like Craig's List, are usually very low budget or free shows, including UCLA Thesis shoots. Don't get drawn in by promises that "the next one" will be a BIG show with proper money. They will NOT call you for the next one, because you are the low budget guy. Do not expect gratitude. The next phone call you get from them will be when they have another micro-budget work-for-credits-and-copy gig.

I know you will want to be working creatively. Be patient and think of your whole career in the long term.

The only internships that are genuinely useful are the official ones organized through your college or the rare union or big company/studio trainee programs. This is because there is an expectation that at least part of the time they will offer actual specialized training to the intern, rather than just assigning grunt labor and stealing your soul.

Otherwise they can call it interning, but it's really working for free on very low budget or student shows, and it can hurt you in the long run. How?

- You get pegged as the free guy by the producers of that show.
- Your resume gets filled up with free gigs, so every other producer knows you are the low budget guy.
- You get into bad habits that come with micro-budget work - or everyone assumes that you have bad habits. (I know - I had them!)
- No-one will trust you with millions of dollars if you have only ever had charge of thousands (or even hundreds).
- In this business, it's **all about your network**. Most people - the vast majority - stay in the network and level where they started. If it is low budget, there you tend to stay, surrounded by everyone you know also stuck in low budget, until you end up leaving the business in frustration.

I strongly encourage everyone starting out in the business to look for work on the highest budget, most prestigious projects that they can find, including internship opportunities with well-known and highly respected people - regardless of how *lowly a position* you take.

"If you are going to sweep someone's floors for free, you might as well sweep Steven Spielberg's."

Once you have graduated from film school, I discourage you from working for free on student films and micro-budget projects - unless you already have a prior personal connection with the director or producer, or the project itself is truly intriguing and different (probably festival bound). The summary is "don't do it for career reasons- it's only worth it for personal ones." But remember – every minute, and all the emotional investment that goes along with it, that you give to that project, is a minute you aren't devoting to finding a real gig.

But what about low budget? By that I mean less-than-one to four-million-dollar fodder for basic cable or direct-to-DVD/streaming (video as it used to be when Blockbuster still had brick-and-mortar stores), that expects to make its money back on international distribution over time.

This was the milieu where I started - and finished! Some people, like Roger Corman for example, have made a fantastic career and gained notoriety because of what they have successfully achieved at these low, low budgets. A good part of their success is volume; just like selling any inexpensive product, you make money when you sell a lot of them. One way that they save money is through using "interns", recent grads and people new to the business, whose rates are lower. There are a lot of people who started with Roger Corman and moved on up - but there are also many more who never gained a foothold in higher budget productions. It's a high churn business for personnel.

I worked for a different low budget company that pushed out serviceable, formulaic, but still entertaining, thrillers. They often had two shooting at once. I had been designing for while at rock bottom rates. The first time I asked for a small pay raise on the next movie, on the strength of prior smart, money-saving work for the company, I was let go. Wages and personnel fees are one of the biggest line item costs in making any movie - and I would go so far as to say that in low budget films they assume an even greater proportion of the final budget.

There is never enough money on these projects to fully realize anyone's vision, but you always try. That's where the heartbreak comes in.

One of the problems with working in low budget consistently is that you get into the habit of being frugal, up to the point that your ideas start staying small. Even when there might be more budget available, your ideas can stay stuck. It doesn't occur to you to pay an artisan to build something amazing, because you become used to cobbling something together yourself. Sometimes it works out well, and you have a moment of pride in knowing that the amazing looking stairwell was your clever cardboard and sticky tape contrivance in a closet. However, there is always that caveat – "it looks great, *for a low budget movie*."

In low budget compromises are constant, starting with the script. The original vision might be for a complex multi-location montage - but you end up having to settle for one establishing exterior shot and a single set up. There were many times when I stood with the Director and Producer and outlined the costs (pared to the bone) of creating two sets, but we didn't have the budget for both, so I asked them to pick which had the most value to the story.

Often locations were chosen based almost entirely on price. New filmmakers quickly use up all their favors with their friends - using friends' homes, gardens and garages as locations for free. But even with paid locations, the ones that are the lowest price are often only "almost right." I remember the time on-set dressing, I was asked to "hide the swimming pool" outside the picture window because it was too luxurious for the character. I managed it with a lot of judicious moving of potted plants and some sleight of hand. Being in an "almost right" location restricts what every department can do, especially what shots can be designed.

There is the pervasive belief that low budget = restrictions = more creativity. That *can* be true, especially in the context of creativity exercises. Also, people doing design work always appreciate a clearly delineated brief. But I notice that this pro-restrictions idea is espoused chiefly by people hoping to justify making movies without proper budgets, to draw you in to work for them for free.

It does take extraordinary creative thinking to come up with ways around limitations, to come up with good, innovative solutions in the face of restrictions. So, what happens when the creative thinking is ordinary, run-of-the-mill, not particularly new? In other words, what if you are in the low budget rut? Your ideas have become small, easily repeatable, because "how much will this cost?" has become your *first* question.

The budget is in the details. Watch any reasonably budgeted movie and look for the transitional scenes. These will be moments when a character is walking somewhere, parts of a montage, establishing shots, moments. They add to the richness, the veracity, the atmosphere, the milieu or our understanding of the character, even if there is little added to the story. These 1/8 page moments in unique sets are the first things to disappear from a low budget shooting script.

Count the set ups in a scene. These cost money, because they cost time. In low budget they can't afford the time for many different set ups.

Nor can you afford in low budget to waste money on things that may not be shot. This particularly applies to Art Department. Often it means pre-planning (which is good when it works) - but it also means having to say no to the Director (awful feeling) or as happens more often, having to cobble something else together on the spur of the moment (one of my fortes as an On-set Dresser I'm almost sorry to say) when they realize on the day that they really do want more angles for the scene.

One of the great tricks in low budget filmmaking is to write a juicy minor character - limited locations, limited shoot days - that will appeal to a more established star. Star power is huge in marketing/promotions. The star might be someone a producer knows or has a connection to, who will support the project for their own "giving back" reasons. Or it might be that the value such a star brings, the star's cache, is worth devoting a substantial portion of the budget to that one shoot day.

Stars do bring value. They may even be willing to do a bit of publicity for the film - especially if you can shoot a sit-down interview on the set the same day they come in to shoot their 1 1/4 pages.

But here's the thing - the production value and quality must match the aesthetic value of the Star - not just for the scenes in which the star appears - but for the rest of the movie too. I don't only mean the art department where it is most noticeable - I mean everything - the quality of the writing (if you can write well enough to attract a name for that scene, then do it for the whole thing!), the costuming, the props, the lighting, the acting.

Case in point - I remember when a certain mid-level star (nice man) arrived to do his bit part playing a wealthy crime boss. The Prop Master had a selection of reasonably luxurious watches for the character to wear. The star glanced at the tray, then held out his wrist and said, "How about I wear mine" - a whopping gold and diamond studded Rolex. It made the other perfectly nice-looking watches look like they came from Cracker Jack boxes.

In filmmaking time is a huge factor. Most people with design constraints of some kind - say product designers or engineers creating a new product that must be at a certain price point - tend to take a long time developing their new product. The ingenuity is lovingly developed through many iterations. They take a long time getting it right at Pixar too. In filmmaking, time is most definitely money; in low budget, time is at a premium.

There is a saying that I have found does apply: **Good, Fast, Cheap - pick two.**

In low budget the usual choice is Fast and Cheap - and you make it as Good as you can, settling for "good enough". Eventually the knowledge, deep down, that your work is not as Good as you wish it were, that you are not in a pursuit for Excellence, burns your soul.

We who love filmmaking are all artists, working in our

chosen medium. Love of filmmaking can only sustain you for a while. People get burned out working in low budget consistently because of the constant compromise, the constant diminution of your vision, the constant debates, the constant sighing for what might have been. A cursory check of the IMDb of my low budget movies reveals that only a few of my colleagues from those days are still in the business at all, let alone making a success of their career.

If you are going to work on a low budget film, for whatever reason, it's important to watch yourself for those bad habits creeping in - bad habits of practice and bad habits of thought.

And move on to bigger things as soon as you can.

CHAPTER 9: COLD CALLING

This is a generalized variant of the cold calling script I recommend to my clients. This may be the most valuable section of this book. By cold calling, I mean that you do NOT have a direct referral, nor been invited to submit your resume by a contact.

I hate picking up that 100-pound phone and calling people, especially as a supplicant. But it must be done! Every call is another tiny thread of connection that, even if nothing happens this time, may pay off in the future as you become a "known quantity" and prove your persistence and enthusiasm.

Calling Your Leads

Go through the production listings and find likely shows.

Look closely at the names of already hired crew available on the listing. If you see the name of someone you know dance the happy dance, because you are already ahead of the game. If you know them well enough, call them, congratulate them on the gig, and ask if the show is "still hiring".

If you are not super close but know each other, you could send your resume to them, via the production office email or a hard copy, with a note saying you saw their name. Remind them how you know each other and ask if they would put your resume in the hands of the right person. You should follow up with them.

This is again where ongoing networking is so important. You don't want to be that person that only calls people to ask them for something. Be the person who calls people when you hear about a show crewing up, or a nice event to attend. But in the absence of a personal ongoing connection, the formality of a note to an acquaintance, is better than a call, IMO.

But for now, let's assume that you don't have either a friend on the show, or an introduction of any kind.

Cold Calling the Production Company during Preparation

Be aware that "Preparation" is a vague time when some people might be hired, especially Department Heads, but most of the work is being done on developing the script. There may or may not be cast attached. There may be some location scouting activity, research being conducted by Art and Costume, and a lot of meetings at the Producer level. The project can still collapse and scheduling may be very fuzzy.

However, there are some hints that Pre-production is imminent from the In-Prep listings. If the listed number of Crew already hired is high, including all the department heads - that is a very good sign that the movie will "go" soon. You have more to go on. Be aware that they probably have not yet opened the Production Office for the show (unless it is specifically listed) but are working out of the corporate offices of the Production

Company (big difference).

In general, during Prep is too early to be hired as a PA, or a Post PA. Your calls now are fact finding missions.

Here's a good script for calling a show still in Preparation. Adapt the details to your own words and way of speaking, and practice until it feels natural.

Hi, my name's John Doe. Who am I speaking to?

(Write down the name, if it's odd get a spelling.)

Thanks, [Name]. I'm calling to find out if the production office for [MOVIE TITLE] is open yet.

If you mention the title before the words "production office" they will interrupt you and may shut you down too soon with "the office is not open yet, bye." But you do need to mention the title because many Production Companies work on several pics at once.

There will be a range of answers. With luck the answer will be: "Yes, here's the number." Then you ask this question:

What is the production coordinator's name over there?

(and get a spelling)

The answer may be "No" with a few caveats - it's too early, another month away, the picture is still in development.

Oh shucks, well I'll call back in a couple of weeks then. May I ask for you?

You might get a range of answers - no anyone can help you, two weeks is too soon, that will be fine. The only issue is if the "No" caveat is "the picture is going out of town" in which case you might then ask if it happens to be going to your home town.

Thanks, [Name]. I appreciate it.

Call back in two weeks. The script is essentially the same except you start with:

Hi. This is John Doe calling back. Last time I called I spoke to [name] (or: is this [name]?)

The main point is to be very <u>pleasant</u>, but also make it clear that you are <u>persistent</u>. Therefore, they might as well give you the number of the P.O. and get you out of their hair.

It is rare that someone would say "Don't call back" unless you were stalking - calling back way too soon and too often. Production companies expect these calls.

Sometimes they say that "hiring is complete". This is probably not true if it is still Prep, so you can say something like:

Darn I missed out. I'd still like to send my resume to the production office in case something comes up and you need day players (or: in case anything changes).

Calling the Production Office During Pre-Production.

In Pre-Production, the Production Office folk spend much of their time fielding calls about jobs. Sometimes there will be a recorded message directing you to an e-mail address, or possibly still a fax number. Write that down of course and use the preferred method of contact for your actual resume. Most people use email. They should say if they want the material as an attachment or in the body of the email.

The goals of this call are to be invited to send your resume, and to add a layer of familiarity to your name for when they do see your resume. This is especially helpful if you have already had a couple of conversations with the Company office. ("Oh yeah, this person knows so-and-so over at Corporate.")

Now for speaking to someone. The key here is to have a genuine question to ask so that you have a reason to Press 1 to speak to a real person. Try this:

Hi. This is John Doe. Who am I speaking to?

"This *PA 1*"

Thanks [PA1]. [Name] over at [Production Company] said I should talk to [Production Coordinator's name].

Either they will be available (great) or they won't.

Maybe you can help me. I have the email info from the message, but I wanted to confirm the name and spelling of [the UPM] [or whatever department head you are hoping will see your material.]

Hopefully they are available this early in the morning.

Hi, [PC's name]. I was chatting with [Name] over at [Production Company] and he/she suggested that I call you to confirm the name and spelling of the UPM [or whatever department head you are hoping will see your material] and the email for resumes.

They should tell you this, unless they are being pissy and say, "Just send it to Production". They are less likely to do this if you are asking for the Production Designer or some department that is not a threat to their own job (hence get the PC if possible).

In all honesty if they won't give you a name to which to address your resume, you would do well to find it out from the listing, or even call your other helpful contact back.

Suppose you get the machine with "leave a message" on it, just call back. Don't call at lunch time, or at 5.15pm. Call about 10am, until you get a person.

If the production office opening has been a long time coming, and you have made a lot of calls to the Production Company office you could say something light like:

Hi, [PC's name]. It sure is great to finally be talking to you. [Name] over at [Production Company] and I have been chatting for weeks while we waited for the office to open.

Any time you find a chatty person on the phone, by all means, take advantage of the opportunity to **form a connection**.

Of course, if you have not spoken to the Company office earlier, don't pretend to have. Simply ask to confirm the spelling and correct name.

If they say they are done hiring:

Well shucks. I'd still like to send my resume in case you need day players. Should I email it to your attention?

Alternatively, you could try pushing for a specific department:

I wonder if the Art Department has all the day players they need. Perhaps I could email the Decorator. Do you have their email handy?
Or:
Shucks. Do you suppose they might need some PAs for Post? What's the name of the Post Production Supervisor?

You might get lucky.

This is basically a lead that has gone cold, but do be pleasant. In your email cover thank the PC for their time and ask them to keep the resume on file in case of day playing or openings during production. **Using the phrase "day players" shows you have at least some experience and knowledge.**

Following Up on a sent Resume.

I gotta tell you, this was always my least favorite part of the process. Most often this is the time when I most felt like I was bothering someone, and that if they had wanted me they would have called back already. But that was all in my head. I'm sure that my energy when I made this call resulted in the bad effect!

The truth is that the squeaky wheel will get the grease. A

lot of the time it was the person who called back and followed up that I called in to interview, because they showed that they were keen. Sometimes it truly is just bad timing - if you happen to call right when something else is happening, you might get a short response. Don't take rejection personally, or assume it is permanent.

What I found did **not** help was saying "I'm calling to follow up on my resume." It's really too easy for the other person to say "Nothing yet. We'll call you" or some other brush off.

So, I suggest having a slightly different conversation.

Hi, this is John Doe. Who am I speaking to?

Hopefully someone you already spoke to.

Hi [whoever] again. We spoke last week. I'm calling to find out when you're holding interviews for [job title]. [or: when [name of the department head] is planning on interviewing staff].

Chances are the person will say something about sending the resume, and you will mention that you already sent one, but will be happy to send another if it would help. Hopefully they will be clear about whether they are hiring any more folk right now, or maybe they'll give you an appointment or another time to call.

Here is the where the value of networking shows. Isn't it a thousand times easier to say "Hi, this is John Doe. Mary Brown asked me to call you today about the PA job. Did she give you my resume already?" and "I can come in any time you like."

By the way - one day soon you may well be on the other end of the phone when job seekers call. Please remember what it felt like and be kind. My experience has been that people do keep resumes when they say they will, but generally only for the run of the production.

The Union

Production Assistants are not an IATSE position at this time (International Alliance of Theatrical Stage Employees, Moving Picture Technicians, Artists and Allied Crafts - you can see why we just say IATSE), but every other below-the-line position is. There are low budget films that are non-union, lowish budget films that are signatories to the Low Budget Agreement, and films that are union films. Union films mean that the employer contributes to your health and welfare, and retirement accounts. The Motion Picture Industry Health plan is some of the best coverage out there, and very much worth maintaining your membership for.

There are two unions that are almost always part of any film that is not a student gig or the kind of under-the-radar micro-budget project that I encourage you to avoid. These are SAG/AFTRA - the film and TV actors' union - and the Teamsters - the drivers of the trucks, and a few other crafts. I will say that the Art Department set-dressing truck is usually driven by the Lead Man, at least on non-union shows. I guess it is a special dispensation for this department because cube-trucks can only carry so many passengers, and they need the space for the set dressers.

It is usually pointless to cold call an obviously big budget IATSE film, such as a major Studio production shooting in Los Angeles, because they must fill their open crew positions from people on the available roster, and I can guarantee you that the PAs are all people someone already knows. Keep networking!

To become more than a PA on a union film, you must join the union, but the Locals (the divisions for each department in each region) are not open to all to just join for the asking. Each Local has its own procedures for gaining entry, some more difficult than others. Most of these revolve around doing some number of hours over a certain time period. Always keep all your pay stubs! Some guilds even have nice training programs, such as the DGA (Directors' Guild of America).

If you are working towards higher budget films, eventually joining the union will be something that will become an imperative. One way to get in is to be already working on a film that organizes, "rolls over" or "flips", to become union during production. Often these are shows that are right on the cusp between low budget and not-low-enough.

The place to start to learn about the union is http://www.iatse.net/ which has links to all the Locals.

Writers are represented by The Writers Guild of America (WGA) which has West coast and East coast branches. http://www.wga.org/

Directors and ADs are represented by the Directors Guild of America (DGA) - http://www.dga.org/ . The DGA also reps some UPMs when considered part of the Director's team.

Here's a little tip for all you folk who are working on your union hours via the production office. Always ask that your title be Assistant Production Office Coordinator, or APOC, not "Production Secretary". The former is a proper union designation, while the other is not accepted for the hourly tally. The duties might be exactly the same.

Being listed on the roster is great, but it is no substitute for networking. That should never stop.

CHAPTER 10: JOB INTERVIEWS

Your Personal Presentation - or how to dress for your production job interviews

The dress code in Hollywood is interesting and different from any corporate environment. The most casually dressed, even scruffy looking, person on the set or in the production office is liable to be the Director. One of the advantages of working in film is the casual dress code. The people in the suits and ties are most likely from the Studio - Executive Producers or representing the financiers.

In general, you will have a lot of leeway on the set for comfortable, casual clothes that allow freedom of movement and safe working. But someone interviewing for a production job would tread a line between being well dressed and professional looking for the interview and looking too formal for the job and milieu.

Men

- Don't wear a suit and tie. (Except if interviewing for an Executive Assistant position at a Studio or agency.)
- Don't wear work boots (unless a Grip or Electrician.)
- Don't wear excessively baggy, hanging off your butt, pants - or any extreme fad fashion - unless this a cool commercials

production agency but still be cautious.

- Don't wear flip flops or sandals.
- Don't wear a plaid flannel shirt to the interview (again unless Grip/Electric.)
- Don't wear shorts to the interview - they will be fine once you are working.
- Don't wear a baseball cap - you aren't a Director yet.
- Don't wear a movie tee or a tee with slogans.

The best thing to wear for the interview, as I was advised by a very professional Lead Man a few years ago, is:

*Neat, clean well-fitting jeans, khakis, or cargo pants with a belt.
*A relatively thick cotton plain colored crew neck (or polo) tee-shirt (not an undershirt) with a breast pocket, tucked in if you have the physique.
*Or a clean camp style shirt, with the breast pocket.
*A casual jacket, or a jean jacket, or zippered sweatshirt (not a schlumpy, baggy one) - not a pullover hoodie for the interview, but they will be fine on sets when it's cold.
*Clean, good condition, sneakers or running shoes with socks.
*In your breast pocket - a small spiral bound notebook and a writing implement.

Be clean, shaved (or have neat facial hair) and use an

anti-perspirant deodorant. Carry mints just in case.

Be cautious about your cologne. Some people have allergies.

Women

- Don't wear a formal business dress suit (Except if interviewing for an Executive Assistant job at a Studio or agency.)
- Don't wear work boots (like a Grip or Electrician.)
- Don't wear excessively baggy tees - or any extreme fad fashion.
- Don't wear overly revealing or sexy or girly clothes (if you want to be taken seriously.)
- Don't wear flip flops, sandals or stilettos or very high heels/platforms.
- Don't wear shorts.
- Don't wear a baseball cap - you aren't a Director yet.
- Don't wear a movie tee or a tee with slogans.
- Don't wear any jewelry that jingles (a toughie for me - I love bangles.)

Do wear smart but casual clothes that are simple, understated, clean, comfortable so you can move and well-fitting. I recommend separates ahead of a dress. You are wearing interview clothes, not set work clothes.

*Well-fitting (but not super tight) jeans - or khakis, or plain pants - nice cargo pants are good - or a simple skirt - not too short and full or you look girly instead of serious.

*A well-fitting blouse (a tailored white shirt is standard) or top.

*A neat cardigan or casual jacket.

*Low heeled pumps or flat closed toe shoes (boots in winter), or clean running shoes with the jeans.

*If you wear jewelry - simple necklace and earrings, one bracelet (no jingles.)

*Simple makeup (if you wear it) - do not try to look like an actress.

*A simple small purse, and your paperwork in a folio. (Leave your huge tote bag in your trunk.)

*Carry a small notebook and writing implement.

Be clean, neat hair, and use an anti-perspirant deodorant. Carry mints just in case. Be cautious about perfume. Some people have allergies.

If you are unsure about what to wear, look at the company website and examine any candid photos of people at work, especially the people who would be your supervisors. You want to look like you fit in with company culture - but also that you have made an effort for the interview, even if they are very casual on a day-to-day basis. If you want to be sure, you can do a reconnaissance mission and observe the workers coming and going (watch out for casual Friday!). For jobs in development, in a distribution company or any kind of business office job in entertainment, the more usual advice about a businesslike presentation most likely applies but do your research!

What about movie tee shirts - especially as homage?

Be careful! You definitely don't want to wear something that reminds people of a film where they didn't have a good time, even if the project was successful. You may want to offer homage to the Director, but you probably won't be interviewed by him for the entry level jobs. Relationships and history are strange things.

And wearing a tee from some other person's film - just why? What if you happened to wear something that the UPM absolutely hated for some reason? Do your research and maybe save the homage until later.

The Interview

When you first arrive, 5-10 minutes early, have your business card out and ready to hand to the receptionist/PA greeting you. Say your name, if you have a referral that you are an associate of that person, and who your appointment is with (if you know it - otherwise say the job. I like to say the person's name, because it makes the whole thing more personal) and the time of your appointment. Also, ask the receptionist's name, and use it a couple of times.

Chances are they will offer you a bottle of water, maybe even coffee. Politely decline. If you should happen to spill it, you look like a klutz. You could be taking a sip just when someone asks you a question. Plus, if you do drink a bottle of water, you could end up needing the restroom halfway through the interview and that is an uncomfortable vibe to give off. For the same reason, I recommend avoiding pullover sweaters or hoodies - because of how awkward it is to take them off over your head, if you start to feel warm. If you end up leaving them on because of that, you then could perspire effusively, which gives the unwanted impression of extreme nervousness.

Turn off your phone and leave it in your pocket. Do not be busy texting when they call you in, and definitely, don't take any selfies in the lobby! Most productions expect a high level of discretion. It is best not to put even a shadow of doubt in their minds.

Have three or four extra copies of your resume, cover letter and references list available to hand out. While it is true that they could make a copy of the one you sent for any extra interviewers, having extras ready shows your thoughtfulness.

Research and be familiar with the work of the Director, and if possible the UPM and other Producers on the show. You won't be showing off your knowledge unasked, but you must able to answer if they ask you if you have heard of that person's work. It also affects how you will express your skills – a maverick who shoots on the run and values out of the box solutions needs to hear about your quick thinking; a traditional auteur studio director will want to hear about your attention to detail, calm demeanor and stamina.

Read over your own cover letter before the interview. They will most likely ask you questions about your prior work, and yourself. If they are good interviewers, the questions will spring from your res and CL. Especially be ready to reiterate how you know or met whoever it was that referred you for the job.

Otherwise they will probably say the annoying "tell me about yourself." Have that answer ready, an extended version of the elevator pitch, focusing on career issues, rather than your whole life story. You should bring up any unique things about yourself - but not too much that is entirely personal. Don't go back beyond the last few years. (Exception: A person who had some unique achievement as a kid might say it then, to make them memorable.)

Remember, in sales it is not enough to describe the features of the product; you also lead the customer to see the benefits to themselves of those features. When you **practice your answers** to questions, always add a benefit to the feature.

For example, when you note that you were a PA on a

student film, mention that you were chosen to wrangle 40 extras on that short, _because_ you are super-organized and patient. Chances are that you had to wear many hats on your own student thesis film, or during your internship. Mention what characteristics helped you with your duties – unruffled and calm, quick study, organized, ability to transition and then focus – or what general skills you learnt and have now mastered – paperwork, research, invoices, local knowledge.

Remember, a real movie production will hire specialists in each department, so the fact that you operated the camera well on a couple of your student films is not relevant to a PA job. But the fact that you were dependable, and dedicated to the team success, and did whatever was needed to ensure it, is!

If you are interviewing as a runner, they will almost certainly ask you if you have a reliable car. The answer should be an unqualified yes. If you only have access to your mom's, that is a potential problem, so don't volunteer that info, and try to remedy the situation as soon as possible. You should also have proper car insurance.

I have interviewed with directors whose main concern was telling me all about the project, rather than learning anything about me. I have had directors act the whole script out for me - quite entertaining. On one hand, this is good because many of your questions will be answered. On the other hand, you get the feeling they are using you for pitch practice and have no intention of hiring you. This probably happens less to someone interviewing at entry level. Usually you will be interviewed by the UPM or Line Producer, and they tend to be busy, straightforward people.

But this does bring me to: jot down anything important that they tell you in your notebook.

When they ask "any questions" the tendency is to want to ask immediately about money. Of course, this is something you want to ask about, if it has not been mentioned already. However, I recommend having a list of questions (not about the stars which makes you sound like a stalker) ready in your mind - and practiced aloud in advance - for what has not been covered:

- You will want to know about the schedule - when they will be starting principle photography, and when they want you to start:
    - 5 or 6-day weeks?
    - 10 or 12-hour days? Will there be overtime?
    - How long is the shoot?
- Location or sets?
    - In the Zone or distant locations?
- For planning purposes, how much of shoot will be nights?
- You might ask about the size of the crew.
- Then you can ask the financial questions - what pay are they offering, any benefits or kit rentals (if appropriate to the position), mileage allowances or gas (if you are running).

- Ask when they expect to make a decision, and whether they will call you *either way*, or if you should call back on a certain day.

If they have already covered everything that you would have asked, and they say "any questions?" don't just say "no" - go over it again (referring to your notebook if needed) as short recap:

- "Well, you answered all my questions about the schedule and locations, you filled me in on the pay and benefits, and you told me you would let me know of your decision by this date, so I have no more questions. Thank you."

Ask for the job - make the last thing you say that you enjoyed meeting them, and that you would very much like the job (if that is true).

What if the pay is just ridiculously low? There is debate about whether you should negotiate now, or after they have offered you the gig. You should use your best judgment. If you feel the interview went very well, you could try saying something like, "Is that the very best you can do?" when they tell you the hourly or daily rate. But do be sure that this is lower than would be usual at the budget level.

If you feel like they do want you, and it's a great opportunity, you could try saying something like, "I really want to be part of this production, but that pay is a little less than I need. It's not a deal breaker, but is there any way we could find some way to raise it, maybe up the kit rental a bit?" Sometimes they will pay a bigger kit rental because it is easier than calculating taxes and all that other stuff from the wages.

Or you could try negotiating for a longer job, such as segueing into a Post PA position after principal photography is done, expressing that you are confident that you will do a good job and justify staying on. Once I agreed to work for free as a Scenic Painter on condition that I got to work on the On-set Dresser (paid) during the shoot. I became that Designer's go-to On-set Dresser, and never "interned" again - although in all honesty if I were starting over with what I know now, I would have been seeking Art Department PA work with much higher budget shows, including making similar offers. How I did I meet that Designer in the first place, even though I was new in town? I was introduced by someone I met on another movie out-of-town, who knew someone in the production office, just when they were anxious to find labor for the Art Department.

Finally, as you are leaving, now is the time to ask the receptionist for that drink (if they offered and don't look busy in the middle of stuff) - "I'd love that bottle of water now please." This has the psychological effect of making that person invested in you, and it gives you the opportunity to have the last thing you say, for which you will be remembered, be, "thank you, [NAME]. I appreciate it."

Thank the receptionist by name and say goodbye, "I hope I see you again" - even if there were no refreshments involved.

Follow Up

Stand out from the crowd. Immediately afterwards send a hand-written card thanking the interviewers by name, for their time. Do this even if they already told you no, or if you don't intend to accept their offer. There is always the next picture. If you want the job, be sure to reiterate your interest in your short note. You can carry the stamped, addressed envelopes with you, ready to write out the note and get it in the mail at once.

New Trends in Job Interview Practices

With the rise of ATS providers, and "social recruiting" which relies on understanding a candidate's potential through their participation in corporate private social networks, as well as LinkedIn and similar sites, there are some new trends in job interviewing.

The first is that the process can be extended to include one or more pre-interviews by phone. It is just as important to have practiced your answers and elevator pitches for the phone as for the face-to-face interview. Most of the time a phone interview will be scheduled in advance. Here are some tips.

- Smile - it shows in your voice. Don't try to speak too fast and get breathless.

- Do let them know if you are thinking over your answer. It is ok to say, "That's an interesting question" or "I'll have to think about that. Let's see..." to give yourself a moment.

- Some people say that psychologically you are more ready to work if you are dressed and have shoes on, even for a phone interview. Being dressed for work can make you move differently and sit up straighter. Also, they might say, "Can you come right in for the next phase?" Or "Can we call you back via Skype in 5 minutes?" Do you want to say you need more time, just because you have to shower, shave and dress?

- Have your resume and cover letter to hand for reference. The interviewer will most likely have it in front of them too.

- Have a notebook and jot down the person's name, even if you have to ask for a spelling, and use it a couple of times as appropriate.

- Remember to thank them, and ask what the next step will be, and when, and express your ongoing interest in the job (if true). **Send an email thank you note afterwards**.

Another trend is a Facetime or Skype video interview. This means that you should not only pay attention to your own personal presentation, but that of your environment. **Please watch out for your backgrounds**. Don't have piles of laundry on the unmade bed behind you, or a sprinkling of random paper clutter. You know it's the carefully collated research for your next essay, but to the prospective employer it just looks like you're disorganized. Any kind of clutter always looks worse on camera. Don't believe me? Take some photos. People get "clutter-blind". Photos don't let it hide.

Try not to have a plant "growing" out of the top of your head or unfortunate wall art placement. Watch out for reflective surfaces, both for glare and for what might be revealed in the mirror. Basically, be aware and do a test screenshot before the call. Don't end up like those folks we see on the internet with all kinds of inappropriate items showing up behind them.

Have sufficient light so that the interviewer can see your face clearly. Natural filtered light - like a window with a sheer curtain - is best. Avoid strong backlight that will throw your face into shadow. Check the framing.

For audio issues, close the window against noise that you probably aren't aware of any more, like the rumble of traffic. Let others in your household know that you will be on camera and unavailable and ask them not to be noisy.

Plan on being properly dressed, just as if you were going to their office in person.

When you are in an interview room, you might make notes

in your notebook and sometimes refer to it. In that situation, the interviewer can see your notebook. However, on Skype referring to your off-screen notebook can look like you have become distracted, nervous, or are staring off into space.

I recommend that you lift the notebook/clipboard into view of the camera and mention that you are going to "make a note of that", as well as bringing it into view when referring to it in your recap.

Test tasks

Applicants, especially to production office or Studio jobs, are often asked to complete some kind of test task. This might be breaking down a scene but is most often providing coverage of a script. You may even be asked to pitch an idea, again depending on the job. Do your best work and try to hand it in early rather than last minute.

Don't know much about "coverage"? Primarily it is *story* analysis. One of the best books about script coverage and being a Reader, is the classic "Reading for a Living" by T.L. Katahn. It is worth reading for anyone starting out in the business.

Safety

Every now and then, you will be asked to attend a job

interview in a hotel room, or what looks like private home or apartment. Sometimes lower budget shows rent apartments for their production offices, using the bedrooms as offices. Usually you will be relieved to see the living room set up as a reception area, and a few people coming and going. Sometimes the Director and Producer have come from out of town to hold job interviews and a hotel is the most cost-effective short-term option.

If you feel iffy about an address, bring a friend with you, and ignore the rule about turning off your phone. If it feels weird or off when you first arrive, don't go in, then call and tell them you need to cancel because you just accepted another job offer. Don't compromise your safety for the sake of a job interview.

Honestly, I hope you are going to interviews on projects with sufficient budgets to rent proper production offices.

CHAPTER 11: BEYOND ENTRY LEVEL

Studio, Network and Production Company Gigs

Jobs and internships at these corporate entities are usually advertised. Some may even be head-hunted, which is one reason to keep your LinkedIn profile updated. In general, these are less production crew jobs, but more support jobs including in development, casting, and administrative support. These often list past production experience as a "preferred" or "desired" quality.

As listed jobs, most of the time the application will be via an online form. Increasingly these enable you to link your LinkedIn and will often have a place to indicate your connections within the company. You should use your ATS optimized resume, with your properly formatted credits at the end where the human reader will find them. (I also like to include them within duties as I explain in the Chapter 14.)

Tip: For an online application always fill out *every* question/box, including the ones marked "optional". Use the "Comment Box" for your customized cover letter.

Keeping Current

I have had some clients recently, both from within entertainment and in other industries, who had been employed for over 15 years with the same company, with some over 20 on the same show. They approached me because resumes and job hunting have changed some in the interim since they started work. I helped them, of course, but finding commensurate work in film or television has been tough for some of them.

Even when you have a great long-term job, it is a good idea to incorporate some of the strategies that freelance contractors use every day.

Keep networking beyond your immediate colleagues. Don't tie all your prosperity to one star or a small group of individuals. Stay involved in outside projects, your own and other people's, including taking occasional sabbaticals to work on them if you can. Stay vibrant, relevant and connected to others.

You might consider having an exit strategy after a certain amount of time, and build towards that, rather than living at the whim of someone else. People retire, or move on, sometimes suddenly. You don't want to be left high and dry should your show runner decide to move on or your show get axed.

Box/Kit Rentals

Most production crew positions include box or kit rentals in the deal. This is to enable crew members to use and maintain their own tools. For production office workers, this might include one's laptops or tablets. For some jobs, your cel phone is included in the kit, especially if you are using it as a camera. For other crew, there are small hand tools, drills, work gloves and so on.

Runners, or anyone who travels around on behalf of the production, such as Art Department Buyers or Location Scouts, will also be paid mileage for the use of their cars. If you use your car for work, that can be a Federal tax deduction. It is best to keep impeccable mileage records, even if you are being reimbursed for gas. A portion of your car maintenance costs may also be tax deductible.

Start keeping good records now, including of your equipment inventory. The Production Office will often want a copy of that for their files, and it is important for insurance purposes. My husband once lost almost everything when the camera truck carrying his sound equipment to a distant location caught fire on the road, but it was all covered and noted on his spreadsheet.

Additionally, you can claim purchases of equipment used on your job as Federal tax deductions, either as a single deduction, or a depreciating asset. You will be asked about the percentage work use of the tool or item. Keep receipts and records for that reason. You can also claim most job-hunting expenses such as membership on job listing networks or production listing services, or this book.

Department heads, such as the Production Sound Mixer, will typically have personal rental accounts with different vendors, as well as owning their own equipment. They will increase their income by renting to the production.

Career Paths

It's no secret that most people enrolling in filmmaking courses these days want to be Directors, by which they tend to mean of Feature Films. Using someone else's money to make personally relevant, well received, hopefully financially successful, films that express their artistry, is the ultimate goal for many aspiring auteur Director/Producers.

Director is not the only film career possible. For every Director, there are hundreds of other artists, crafts people and technicians working the project. It might be argued that statistically, the best career path is towards something other than Directing, in terms of the likelihood of successfully making a living with longevity in the business. Every department has a Department Head. Every Department Head has an assistant and a staff of specialists and generalists. Everyone started somewhere.

Here is an incomplete list of some of the paths to popular careers in film production. As technology changes and new platforms for distributing content arise, more job designations and specialties also appear. Twenty years ago, there was no such position as "Drone Operator" and the idea that anyone could watch a feature film, let along make their own movie, with their cel phone was an impossible dream. At the same time, some jobs never go away, even if the tools change. I encourage you to search and read about all the positions that you will see on the credits of a film or TV show, to learn more and find your niche.

Feature Film Director

TV is often called a "Producer's Medium", while Film is called a "Director's Medium". TV Series in all genres, usually have a rotating roster of Directors, who may shape the shots and performances to varying degrees, but always within the existing frameworks and pre-planned story arcs. These have been decided by the Producers and Writers, especially the Show Runner who leads the production team, and is often the creative force behind the concept. When people say they "want to direct", most of the time they are talking about Feature Films, where the Director's vision is the leading impetus. However, directing TV is one path towards directing films.

One of the most likely or common paths is via Writing. Writers with either an awesomely-original-but-still-accessible idea or a proven track record of excellence may get the opportunity to direct their own script.

Another traditional method is to come up through the DGA ranks, from PA through several steps to AD (often eventually including Associate Producer credits), and sometimes as UPMs. With this kind of network, you can end up with enough contacts that you get to Direct a feature – possibly after directing Second Unit for your mentor.

A third path is sideways from another related department. Most commonly that is Cinematographer or DP. Next to the Director, the DP has the most influence over the film in terms of the shots, the coverage, and the material that will be handed to the Editor. A good DP, with a track record, might be given the chance to direct, especially if they bring a script discovery to the attention of the production company. Some Directors continue to shoot as well.

Sometimes Editors will be given a break – especially if they have a history of saving films with their cleverness. One way to be clever is to be fast enough putting together a scene to come back with "We need a shot of thus-and-such" before the company has left that set.

Of course, there are also actors who want to Direct, and often do get their chance once they have their own success as actors. Sometimes their opportunity is tied to acting in the same film.

Directors need to know about lenses, filters, cameras and shot types, editing, visual storytelling and the fundamentals of writing. You need to understand the conventions of film narrative, the Hero's Journey, Three Act Structure, archetypes and pacing. You should study classic and modern literature, film history, and communication. A grounding in psychology, acting theory and methods would be helpful, so that you have a common language with actors. I recommend reading Stanislavski, Stella Adler, Sanford Meisner and Lee Strasberg. Reading comic books and graphic novels (at least good ones) is one way to gain an intuitive understanding of using shots to tell stories.

Cinematographer

The Cinematographer or Director of Photography is the head of the camera department. This person works most closely with the Director in supporting the theme and telling the story, and other than the Director has the greatest influence on the look of the final film, arguably even ahead of the Production Designer, especially in lower budget pictures. A good DP collaborates closely with the Production Designer and Costume Designer early on, so that out of that relationship comes even better ideas and innovative solutions to storytelling or practical/technical problems.

The DP is responsible for framing and lighting the shots to create a coherent style and tell the story. Actors will shoot a fast glance to the DP at "Cut" to see if the take itself was good. DPs make actors look more beautiful than they are. Second Unit DPs win the Cinematography Oscar® nominations for their films, with sweeping location vistas and moody establishing shots.

Cinematography has had a huge influence in style and genre, for example Film Noir and Cinemascope. The DP chooses lenses and filters for each shot, as well as the size of the shot –

close-up, wide angle, zooming in or out, panning.

The rest of the camera department are Camera Operators, although many DPs also operate A camera during principal photography, the First AC, who used to be called, descriptively, the Focus Puller, and the Second AC or Loader. The Loader's job has been changing as filmmakers move away from using actual film to digital, but often still includes keeping track of paperwork, and working the slate (clapperboard) – which is usually digital and programmed by the Sound Mixer. A new position in the department is a Drone Operator or Programmer, operating tiny flying cameras by remote control. Specialty areas include IMAX filming, and working underwater. DPs can find themselves on cranes, up ladders, and riding mobile/auto rigs.

The DP instructs and works closely with the Gaffer, who is the head of the Electric Department, and the Key Grip, and Dolly Grip, who is in charge of the rolling rig on which the camera is mounted for moving ("dolly") shots.

The job path could be starting as a grip or electrician on the set or focusing on camera at film school, rather than directing. From there you could move to firstly Second AC, then up to First, a Second Unit Camera Operator, through Camera Operator and finally DP. It is an apprenticeship process. You would want to keep abreast of new camera developments and lighting instruments, including attending seminars given by vendors and industry expos. You would want to read the journals of the

Cinematographer Society and related departments' guilds, study light, learn about depth of field, lenses and filters, study your film history of course, and watch a lot of movies. You could start with still photography to learn about framing and composition, study the Elements and Principles of Design, and certainly play around with video cameras, and phone cams.

Production Designer

The Production Designer, called Art Director in Television, leads the Art Department. They collaborate closely with the DP and the Director to design the overall visual style of the film, particularly focusing on the sets and locations, and work with the Locations Manager on a host of stylistic and practical concerns. They also collaborate closely with the Costume Designer, to ensure that everything fits into the overall concept.

The staff that report to the Production Designer include the Art Director, who oversees anything that will be built (and has a team), the Set Decorator, who selects all the furnishings and wall coverings of the sets, and the Property (Props) Master, who is in charge of any item that the actor touches or uses, including weapons. The Production Designer collaborates closely with the Special Effects (SFX) designers, and increasingly, the CGI team.

There is also an On-Set (or Stand-by Set) Dresser, who moves furniture depending on the shot, watches continuity and acts as the liaison between the action on the set and the PD and Decorator - who will usually be off working on the next set during

Principle Photography. Then there will be a host of other people who report to either the Decorator or the Art Director. The Props Master might hire a Weapons Master, while the Decorator would hire Drapers, Greens people and the Lead Man and set dressing team.

The job path that I took was to have studied and worked in Theater Design, then up through scenic painting and On-set Dresser, to Decorating for a couple of Production Design mentors, to being able to design myself. Other paths could be via construction to Art Director, or from being a Set Designer. In film that is a draftsperson who creates blueprints and construction diagrams, so learning AutoCAD and other drafting programs is a plus. It is not just major sets that might be drafted, but also set pieces or props that need to be constructed.

People who have drawing skills might come to Production Design via Concept or Storyboard Artist. The Art Department often has an Art Department Coordinator to help keep everything organized, researchers, and Buyers who source all kinds of items from industry and other places, bringing back images from which the Decorator, PD and Director choose the best look.

Aspiring Production Designers should study the Elements and Principles of Design, basic drafting, history of architecture, textiles and furnishings, art history, and history in general. They should understand basic construction techniques and something about the unusual materials used in film and theater construction, like sprayed foam. They should know psychology. It is helpful to know about space planning and ergonomics. It is useful to know about costume design, the history of clothing and jewelry also.

Production Designers have got to be able not just to come up with the visual ideas, but also to communicate those ideas to the Director, DP and others. They should enjoy research, and be able to sketch, and give strong attention to detail. Other useful skills include making miniatures, construction, scenic painting and sewing. The other side of the job is estimating and keeping track of the budget and being able to look at a plan and estimate the time and materials needed. It is also useful to be a competent still photographer, especially for putting together your portfolio.

Above: One of my portfolio shots from *Man of Her Dreams* (1996)

Editor

The Editor is responsible for cutting the movie, which is to say joining the different shots into scenes and scenes into the whole story. The action of "cutting" comes from the old days of movies shot and projected on film, where the film stock itself was cut and then joined together until finally the "Negative Cutter" cut the chosen shots and frames from the original negative itself and joined the pieces so new prints of the film could be made for distribution.

The Editor usually has at least one Assistant, as well as people like Loggers and administrators or office people working for them. Editors often work through their own Post-Production companies, which also offer all kinds of other Post Services including Foley, Sound FX and related editing, and visual FX. Today much of this entails seamlessly integrating CGI with the shot footage. Editors report to the Director regarding creative feedback, and the Post Production Supervisor (the Post equivalent of a the UPM) for practical matters.

Editors must have an impeccable understanding of story, timing, and genre. They must be patient and enjoy repetitive work. Often, they are introverts who don't mind spending time alone, but they must also be able to listen and communicate creative concepts. They collaborate most closely with the Director. They must be able to visualize strongly from reading a script. A good Editor will transcend the script and bring even more to the story.

They also need a thick skin, and the ability to absorb and act on criticism without taking things personally. Editors are in the lucky position of being able to express their ideas visually, and then go back to square one with no harm done if the idea doesn't fly.

One path to Editing is through starting as a Post PA or logger and working as an Assistant Editor for a Post-Production facility. You should show yourself to be reliable and fast, so that you will be given scenes to work on, and later the shorter or less interesting projects that come through the post house. Then eventually you will be able to do larger projects. Alternatively, you could do what Steven Rifkin did and set up your own editing suite with your own equipment and start with commercials and industrials. However, he did have prior film production experience before taking that step. So, working as a PA and learning the ropes is a good idea.

You should read as many relevant film journals as you can, keep abreast of the technical advances in the equipment and software for editing, practice on your own films, and consider specializing. Documentaries are made in the Editing room. You might also start as a writer and should certainly be interested in storytelling. Musicians, who have a strong understanding of pace, can make good Editors, and Editors will often collaborate with the Sound Designer/Re-recording Mixer.

Production Sound Mixer

The Production Sound Mixer is responsible for recording all dialogue spoken by actors to capture their verbal performance, including wild lines (off camera lines), and collecting room tone from each set or location. Room tone is the ambient sound of a place, that becomes an underlying unifying sound as part of the final mix created in post. It is especially important if any dialogue must be "looped". Also called ADR (Additional Dialogue Recording), this means the actor comes to recording stage and tries their best to recreate their performance, lip synching to their image on screen. There's always some, but a good Production Sound Mixer does all they can to minimize the need, including pointing out avoidable noise pollution, like noisy refrigerators or the generator positioned too close the set.

Mixers choose the appropriate microphones, including determining if a shot should have a wireless mic or be boomed, or be a mix of the two feeds. Additional responsibilities include managing the headsets for the Director, Script Supervisor and others in the video village watching the shots. They will also program the smart slate that synchs the audio recording with the digital camera and incorporates time code to both sets of data (sound and picture). Their other responsibility is synching any music playback, and sometimes recording live music. Other duties include writing up clear Sound Reports, managing rental and insurance paperwork, and supervising their team's time cards.

The Mixer supervises the Boom Operator and the Utility Sound person, once called the "Cable Person". Other careers in the Sound arena are in post - ADR Mixer, Foley Mixer and Foley Artist (Foley is manually created sound effects such as steps, the sound of punches and other odd sounds), Sound FX Editor, Sound Editor, and Sound Designer, who has an over-arching vision and who often mixes/produces all the elements of the sound track including Dialogue, FX, background sounds and Score.

Most Production Sound Mixers have come up through being a Utility, then Boom Operator. You can study Production Audio and Post Audio, as well as general Recording Arts in college, and apprentice with a working Mixer. Most own at least some of their own equipment and have strong relationships with industry vendors to stay abreast of new technology. You should study auditory physiology, acoustics and microphone/playback technology. A bit of electronics, including how to solder, can be very useful on location. Knowledge of the history of recording as well as the psychology of sounds, such as how certain music effects emotions, can only help you.

For more information about sound mixing and boom operation, please visit http://MovieSoundMixer.com.

Producer

Producers balance the creative side of filmmaking with the pragmatic, financial side. In the end the Producer is responsible for the results of every decision that has been made by every person down the line. A Producer needs vision, and a high tolerance for risk, as well as an ability to multi-task beyond everything else.

Above: James Coburn's Sound Cart

The Producer hires all the Department Heads, beginning with the Writer and the Director. Sometimes the Producer will have the idea and hire a Writing team to put it on paper. At other times, they will see the potential in an existing screenplay or idea, option it, and move forward into Development. They put together the "Package", which includes the stars, and plan the overall distribution and marketing strategy in collaboration with specialists in those fields. They source and manage the entire budget, production and post, and often have to justify or defend their project to their own financiers or Studio/Network heads. Often there will be several Producers on a project, and the work will be divided according to individuals' particular strengths or passion.

Producers tend to have a strong rolodex of contacts and past crew members. For many, their purpose is to take care of the practical, everyday production needs to free the Director from having to worry about them. At the same time, sometimes the Producer has to keep the Director focused and on track.

Speaking as a writer, having a good creative Producer who understands story and structure, who can communicate feedback clearly, is a wonderful boon.

The paths to Producer are many. Some come via Production, moving up through ranks from Production Coordinator to UPM to Line Producer. Others rise through the ranks at production companies or Studios, particularly starting in Development. Producers who find spectacularly original writers or hit upon a great franchise idea that finds success, will rise swiftly.

Other Producers come from the financial side, with MBA's or a past record of brokering connections between people with money, who want to invest in film, and creative companies. They might then add the creative aspects of Producing after gaining experience. Increasingly, film schools are offering Producing strands for film and television. In Television, the lead Producer is called the Show Runner, and is often the originator of the series idea. They may have been a Writer in the past.

It is important to understand of all aspects of production, and especially be able to determine a budget. It is good to know about Distribution, markets and the technical aspects of deals. You should stay abreast of trends in the industry, including reading the Trades assiduously. You will have to deal with all kinds of volatile and creative personalities, so knowing a bit of psychology wouldn't hurt. The best Producers are team builders, with enormous energy and encyclopedic knowledge of the business, and an ability to cultivate relationships.

Writer

There is an old saying: "If it's not on the page, it's not on the stage." Everything starts with the Writer, but it is one of the hardest jobs to make a success of. There are hundreds of screenplays and teleplays languishing in the bottom drawers of their writers' filing cabinets, even if they have been registered with the WGA.

Here is a little-known fact. Most working screenwriters earn most of their income from writing-for-hire from a Producer's idea, and re-writing existing projects which may never be produced, rather than finding success with their original spec script or pilot idea. Far more writing is done for projects "In Development" than in Production. Existing TV series have a team of writers who all pitch ideas and stories that must fit in with the overarching plan devised by the Story Editor and Show Runner. Consider a spec episode to be a writing sample, rather than something with any reasonable chance of being produced. Meanwhile, everyone you meet will "have a script" they are either working on or trying to sell. I have several.

At the same time, the Writer is one of the easiest people to replace, once they have completed their contract. Most movies have several writers, and one of the primary activities of the WGA is settling credit disputes. They have people who do nothing but count words and compare drafts all day long. This is far more frequent than work or ideas being "stolen", which many new writers worry about to a far greater degree than reality warrants.

There is a huge wealth of books, magazines, courses and creative writing degrees out there, as well as conferences, contests and events, to help you learn how to be a better writer and make a success of your career. Some come to writing from being a Reader in the business (as mentioned in the last chapter), while others work in another department and start writing when they have an idea. Some screenwriters come from other areas of writing, including genre fiction.

Read screenplays and great literature and understand the proper formats and film conventions. Study genre, three act story structure, the Hero's Journey, archetypes and film history.

The best advice is to keep writing, keep re-writing, and know that the next draft WILL absolutely be better than the last one. Keep networking so that you can get someone to read your work who might be in a position to option it or hire you. As far as contests go, *Caveat Emptor*, and try to read on forums and social media about them before you spend your money on entry fees. The more you write, the better a writer you will become. Grow a thick skin about rejection and feedback, and constantly work to improve, while at the same time, put your work out there. Don't let perfection become the enemy of the good.

Never Stop Networking

Even when you have a great gig and are rising in the business, keep attending screenings, expos, vendor training events, conferences, and film festivals. Keep widening your network of people in the business.

It is not just how helpful this will be for your career, but also for your creativity. Studies investigating creativity show that people who persistently work only with the same few people because it is comfortable, can become creatively stagnant after a while. Change is good!

CHAPTER 12: MY SERVICE

I provide a "done-for-you" resume and cover letter writing service, customization for specific job listings, critiques of your professional website, and evaluation of your design portfolios. My goal is for you to know how to update and customize your own resumes for the future, with confidence.

I also offer a 2-4 hour presentations and workshops to small groups, including individual evaluation and feedback of your resumes, which might be a more cost effective way for groups such as students to learn the process. One of these is entirely about analyzing job listings.

See my website for more details and pricing.

http://www.WorkInProduction.com/myservice

The Client Survey

When we start working together I send you a survey. The answers are especially helpful to me in understanding your goals, and in composing personalized cover letters that do more than merely reiterate your resume content in prose. For more about cover letters, see my book **"Work in Production Part Two: How to write a killer cover letter that the UPM will actually want to read."**

If taken with thought and openness, the survey should help

you drill down to some of the unique traits and experiences that make you memorable and interesting. One person learnt to scuba dive while volunteering in Thailand. Another was a former barista who knew all kinds of tricks for making awesome coffee. Another was a fantastic ping-pong player, which was great to reveal when she interviewed with a company that had a ping-pong table right there in the production office, as we could see from the website. One person was a leader in her high school marching band.

Even defining what you didn't like about certain jobs helps when writing a cover letter. One client hated that she was given very little direction or instruction from her internship supervisor, so she ended up walking around the office offering to help everyone there with all kinds of different tasks. She created a fantastic internship experience for herself, learned many new skills, and highlighted an important personal quality - being self-starter. All of these ideas would go into the cover letter and resume, of course without mentioning her dislike of her supervisor.

You can also use the survey to define your goals for yourself. Here it is. Enjoy.

About You

- Are you interested in Film/TV work or Theater?
- Where and what have you been studying? (Highest educational qualification)

125

- What is/was your favorite part of your studies?
- What is your favorite film or theater genre, and what appeals to you about it?
- What are your hobbies and favorite activities outside of work/school?
- Do you have any unusual skills?
- Do you know how to make coffee?
- Do you own a reliable car?
- What is one whacky or fun thing that few people know about you?

About Your Work

- What was your first job (of any kind)?
- What stands out in your memory about it?
- What other jobs have you worked? Tell me what your responsibilities were? (If you are a veteran tell me about that here.)
- What did you like about the jobs?
- What did you dislike?
- Have you ever been fired? What happened? (No judgment - just a learning opportunity)
- Have you been going to interviews?
- Where have you been finding your leads?

- What kind of networking events do you attend, if any?

Your Future

- What are your long-term career goals – the big ones? Where do you see yourself in 5 years? 10 years? 20 years?
- List three things that you are doing now towards your goals.
- You will consider yourself successful when (your eulogy) ....

The Big Question

- Why show business?

CHAPTER 13: RESOURCES AND LINKS

- People and productions http://www.imdb.com/
- Information site http://www.filmmakingstuff.com/filmmaking/
- Production Listings http://findfilmwork.com/
- Stage 32 Social Networking
  https://www.stage32.com/welcome/21/
- ProductionHUB https://www.productionHUB.com/
- Employment Listings http://www.entertainmentcareers.net/
- A Training program
  http://www.hollywoodcpr.org/training/training.html
- IATSE general site http://www.iatse-intl.org/
- CA Film Commission - many links
  http://www.film.ca.gov/ProductionTools_GuildsUnions.htm
- Networking group http://www.newfilmmakersla.com/
- Great Q&A Legal site http://filmtvlaw.com/entertainment-
  lawyer-qa/ Scroll for awesome info from past questions
- Women in Media networking group – and access to great
  discounts for members on some production services
  http://womennmedia.com

Books - These are ones that I have read. (There are too many
"how to" writing books to list. I recommend looking at the samples
and reviews to find the ones that resonate with you.)

- "The Production Assistant's Pocket Handbook" by Caleb Clark - lots of excellent lingo
- "Reading for a Living" by T.L. Katahn

Magazines I like -
- Script - http://www.scriptmag.com/
- Writers' Digest - http://www.writersdigest.com/
- Movie Maker - http://www.moviemaker.com/
- Cinefex - http://www.cinefex.com/

For fun -
- "The 50 Worst Films of All Time" and "The Golden Turkey Awards" by Harry Medved - hilarious, laugh-out-loud film criticism.
- My site: http://workinproduction.com/
- FB: https://www.facebook.com/WorkInFilm

CHAPTER 14: ATS VS HUMAN

What is an ATS?

ATS stands for Applicant Tracking System, and there are numerous companies that specialize in providing ATS with various capabilities. But the most important feature for job seekers is their ability to sort and rank submitted resumes per specific criteria, including keywords and key phrases that reflect past experience and job duties, and specific formats.

The primary reason hiring companies use ATS is, unsurprisingly, to manage volume. Some jobs will have many hundreds of applicants, and some of those will be submitted by semi-automated job search agencies - computers submitting and trying to beat another computer's algorithms. The way the ATS work means that many perfectly qualified candidates with format errors end up on the No pile, automatically. However, because of the numbers, there will still be 15-20 or more good matches to continue to the next step. The next step still isn't someone reading your resume, but someone looking at the ATS generated summary report which counts the keywords included and the keywords missing.

Despite the ambivalence towards them that HR pros often express, ATS are not going away any time soon. It is best to learn the tricks and "get with the program", so that your resume gets close enough to the top of the pile, to be seen by a person.

To succeed, most resumes should maintain a fine balance between the limited structure ideal for ATS and being readable and interesting for the HR person who will eventually see it. These folks believe that they give resumes their deepest attention, but according to recent eye movement studies, they take a mere 6 seconds to make their evaluation. (It takes 7 seconds to read the preceding sentence aloud at a reasonable pace for a listener.) You have just that long to capture the interest of the human reader before they set your document aside forever. Humans like plenty of white space, variation in texture (Bold or italic used well), clarity and especially layered bullets. They look for metrics - dollar amounts, numbers of clients, time, percentage growth.

The other important place that ATS formatting is used is for **college internships**. If you are a student currently in college or film school hoping to gain a great internship for your degree, you would do well to read these tips carefully. My experience has been that the internship coordinators at colleges are HR trained rather than production trained. They look after students wanting internships in many industries and tend to insist that you format your resume as if it is for an ATS, whether the company offering the internship uses them or not. Often, they do not emphasize credits the way a correct production resume should.

In a situation where the good will of the internship coordinator makes a difference to your access to the

131

opportunities, you should of course, follow their instructions. But do leave the company an updated, properly formatted resume for their files, when your internship is done, along with handwritten thank you notes for your supervisors.

Headings

The first part of office/business resumes used to be the "Profile". This generally consisted of three or four columns listing all the positions for which a person might be qualified, then with some general skills. It was a trend that moved in the opposite direction of successful job seeking, by emphasizing the general rather than the specific. Resumes that start with Profiles often feel like the seeker can't be bothered to write a customized resume - something sadly too true, too often.

When I create a resume for listed jobs, I generally prefer a "Summary" which includes metrics and skills, which can be then be customized to the job listing. My goal is that the person reading the summary wants to reach for the phone to call you even before looking at your Work Experience. You can also use a comprehensive Summary for the Summary section at the start of your LinkedIn Profile.

ATS typically use computer algorithms with narrow parameters that look for key words and key phrases, that are found within the job listings, as well as certain common formats.

Those resumes that are successful, fit in with certain format requirements because the ATS are essentially stupid. For example, they like the heading "Work Experience", *not* "Professional Experience", "Work History", "Employment anything" or any number of other synonymous combinations that a real person recognizes immediately.

They also look for the heading "Education" near the start of the resume, before the work history, even for jobs that are not entry level.

About length

ATS parse content without seeing page breaks, so the length is somewhat irrelevant - although material at the end of a long resume is given less weight in the breakdown scores, because it is assumed to be, and should be, chronological. The general advice today is keep your resume no more than 4 pages for most situations.

Further, having a too short resume can hurt you. Before she started with me, one of my clients had kept her resume to one page by leaving out most of the duties. The young lady who interviewed her almost sneered at it, saying, "I would have expected this to be longer." When I was finished, it was 4 correctly written pages, reflecting her long experience accurately, and she was offered the next job to which she applied with it.

How do you get your resume in front of a human?

Networking!

I know it seems like a short answer, but it is the truth. Networking puts you in contact with people who will invite you to send them (*or their assistant*) your resume.

Online networking can help too. In fact, it is a fast-growing sector of the Human Resources sector overall. Companies have started hiring Social Network facilitators to build private social networks which job seekers are expected to join to learn about new vacancies, instead of jobs being listed. Check out http://www.ascendify.com/ to get an overview of the early adopters of what could be a major new trend. It seems like a natural extension of the success of LinkedIn.

People in your social media circle might visit your website or LinkedIn profile where you keep your resume. Put your production resume on as many of the industry social networking and job lead sites that you can. Remember to update it as needed.

LinkedIn is a search engine. It is important to repeat keywords to raise your profile in the results. Repeat your job title, and repeat the duties for each job, even if it seems boring.

Education

You must have an Education section on your resume, especially for listed jobs. Eye-scan studies show that HR people specifically search for applicant's Education information on the resume, and ATS will look for it specifically and score higher for it, even when a job description specifies a certain level of education "OR" some amount of experience.

Unlike production resumes, for ATS the Education section goes at the top, immediately after the Summary if used.

Customizing - Keywords and Key Phrases

The English language is loaded (crammed, full, crowded) with synonyms for every verb, noun and adjective. In the absence of a job listing with specific keywords, it is helpful to include plenty of commonly used synonyms in your skills and job duties - to cover all bases.

It is not enough just to look at individual keywords either. Increasingly ATS will score based on *key phrases* from the listing being repeated in sensible contexts in your resume (and cover letter too). Sometimes these phrases will be common ideas like "excellent written and verbal communication skills" or just the phrase "communication skills", repeated a couple of times. Sometimes the phrases will be unusual, that speak to the hiring company's self-branding, and only mentioned once, such as "a powerhouse on the phone" or "solid knowledge of workflow" or "diplomatic and tactful". You can't just shoehorn these into the resume but should place them elegantly and appropriately.

Resume writing is one place where it is allowable, if not desirable, to use tautology. That is to say, repeat concepts within a sentence or bullet point with different words whenever possible. E.G. "Strong interpersonal communication ability with excellent written, verbal and presentation skills" or "maintains high level of discretion with proven understanding of confidentiality."

Check what verbs they use. Typical verbs are "manage", "handle", "coordinate" and "organize". The verbs are a clue to the management level of the position. Check whether they use "collaborate" or "work with" for you customizing. In the absence of a listing, use both.

When a resume should show a Skills section, the skills and abilities will usually be drawn directly from the job listing. Always include a descriptor - one of a short list of words (again use the listing as your guide.) Imagine there is a silent "I am a/an...." Or "I have a/an...." before the bullet.

We can generally expect certain common phrases and their synonyms to be used. Nobody minds tautology in resumes.

Skills

Here are typical examples which will be found, more or less, with small variations in many job listings:

- Pro-active self-starter, with strong ability to anticipate needs
- Strong ability to follow detailed instructions and manage complex task sequences
- Outstanding multitasker with strong ability to prioritize and maintain focus as needed
- Excellent cross-functional communicator with strong written and oral [or verbal] communication skills and presentation experience
- Team player with very strong ability to collaborate across functions and departments
- Creative [or quick] thinker with excellent problem-solving [or troubleshooting] skills
- Thrives under pressure in fast paced [or fast-paced] environments
- Highly effective organizer with outstanding time-management skills and strong awareness of deadlines
- Proven fast learner with seeking attitude and flexible mindset
- Highly dependable with excellent record of reliability

- Extremely discreet with strongest possible ability to maintain confidentiality
- Consistently takes ownership of tasks and seeks increasing responsibilities

You would look at the job listing which shows more keywords, key phrases and descriptors to make the changes needed, but this is a good general list. At entry level, there is unlikely to be much about supervising or training others, which would be another bullet point of skills.

Most job listings will specify particular software and will use either "Fluent" or "Proficient". *In the absence of a listing, squeeze in both.* Everyone wants MS Office Suite. Some listings will specify Excel or PowerPoint, so use the wonderful word "including…"

For the most effective ATS resume, you want to insert as many of the skills as you can *within the job duties, even if it is repetitive.* Again, this is unlikely to be for a crew PA gig. But here is an example with the skills underlined for your reference:

*Managed daily calendar and organized weekly meetings, using Google Calendar, with strong attention to detail
*Maintained ongoing awareness of deadlines
*Communicated effectively in writing and verbally with multiple department heads [you could insert a metric here too: some

number of department heads]

More detail about how to analyze a job listing to find the keywords, key phrases and unusual descriptors, and how to customize your resume to the job listing and optimize for ATS will be found in my upcoming book **"Understanding Job Listings: How to Customize your Resume and Cover Letter for Each Job."**

Determining Your Duties from Past Jobs

Many of my clients have a hard time quantifying their duties or getting down to the nitty gritty of them. There is a tendency towards simplicity - because it is easier to write "general office duties" than break that down into specific tasks. Don't get lazy! **Every bullet point is an opportunity to add keywords** and phrases and show your diligence and attention to detail. Plus, people think they are writing to the usual rules of English expression and worry about being repetitive. Repetitive is good on a resume, especially one where a computer will be counting the keywords.

Sometimes it helps to revisit a current job listing for the position you once held, to remind yourself of the many things that were part of your duties. However, if you do not have access to a similar job description, it can be helpful to spend some time mentally walking through a typical day, or week, and then thinking of any special events. Take your time.

Duties can be grouped into areas of responsibility also and expressed using "jobspeak" to make them more transferable. Here are a couple of examples from a past clients.

- Collaborated with Marketing team on special events
- Independently initiated and managed donation of station archives to local college library
  - Operated dub station to convert 200+ DVC tapes to digital format
  - Configured start/stop times; color corrected visuals; adjusted audio levels
  - Organized collection with corresponding written log of all relevant statistics

The above is a good example because it shows the duties done right as well as a missed opportunity. It would have been great to go into more detail about the events mentioned, and the specific responsibilities this client took on in that collaboration. But the library project shows technical tasks and the record keeping involved, as well as a nice metric (200+ tapes). These would be great transferable skills for someone seeking an entry level gig at a post-production house, which is often about logging and transferring tapes.

- Manage day-to-day operation of events department
    - Submit weekly reports to marketing team and management; attend weekly meetings; research and keep current about issues relating to beverage industry
    - Work closely with marketing team to help manage online and media presence; maintain marketing & events calendar and ensure all staff receive updates & details of upcoming events
    - Contribute to website and social media content; update & maintain e-mail lists

That is an example showing the duties of day-to-day operations expanded. Notice the grouping of duties into meetings, marketing and social media outreach. Good additions would be to mention the calendar or other software, to specify the social media sites, and to note the number of subscribers to the email lists.

- Managed administrative tasks to support Department Supervisor
    - Operated acquisitions module to create selection lists and materials orders
    - Handled word processing, database and spreadsheet management

This is a simple expansion of administrative tasks. It could have been improved with some metrics such as the department budget for orders, and maybe a mention of the software used.

Etc.

No, no, no, no. If you want to write "etc.", that means there is more to be said. It means you are tired of thinking about the duties or writing them down. So, take a 10-minute refreshment break, or a walk around the block, and come back to continue.

Every use of "etc." is a missed opportunity to insert a keyword.

Don't assume that anyone will correctly guess what "etc." means.

Don't send up a big, red, "I'm lazy" flag with that horrible word, which has no place on anyone's resume.

Credits on ATS Resumes

Generally, I put the Credits section following the ATS optimized work experience. This might be for an entertainment related job but is unlikely to be a production crew gig. I might bullet crew duties under each credit if they have not been expressed earlier, because the hirer may not be aware of the specifics, and you want to keyword/key phrase load from the listing. This is where "in a timely manner", "pro-active self-starter", "attention to detail", and especially, "multi-tasker" tend to come up.

Often for an ATS resume I will fold the credits in to the relevant past job itself. This works especially well for jobs in Development or Distribution - essentially office jobs but in the industry. The ATS will not understand the gigs, but the human at the next stage will.

DISTRIBUTION CO., Los Angeles, CA   **Film Development Assistant**   *Dec 2015 – Present*
- Read, translate and provide written coverage for scripts in development
- Communicate as needed with writers' agents; prepare option paperwork
- Research and source original material to propose as China-USA co-productions
    - Research intellectual property rights
- Evaluate project packages submitted by strategic partners including production companies
    - Analyze corresponding film market
    - Provide commentary and reports to Executives in charge of production
- Provide administrative support to Distribution Department
    - Organize meeting schedules
- Prepare promotional materials such as posters and print ads for upcoming releases
- Films in Production/Development include: *Film Title One, Film Title Two* and *Film Title Three*

Finding the Names

When sending a job application to a company, especially when they have an online application form to fill in (Answer every single question! Leave none blank), it can be almost impossible to find out the name to which to address your cover letter from the listing. If they have given a name, or you can deduce it from the email address and quick cross reference with the company website, by all means, use it. There is nothing that says "careless" faster than not using the name that you have actually been given, in favor of "Dear Sir/Madam".

Personalizing the salutation is always a good idea. Unless they specify "No calls", you could try phoning and saying that you want to check the spelling of the Department Head or the Hiring Manager's name. Hopefully someone will give you that information. Otherwise you may be able to find the right name from the website.

ATS Formatting Tips

- Use one of the basic simple fonts - Arial, Verdana, Calibri, Georgia, Times New Roman.
- Do not use accents over letters. You will notice I don't use the word résumé with accents in this book. Most ATS, at least in English, cannot parse accents.
- Stay at 11 points or larger - don't try to cram in more information by going smaller. It leads to parsing errors which read as spelling mistakes.
- No underlining - but it is OK to use Bold and Italics to create emphasis. Underlines can confuse the ATS and again lead to the appearance of spelling errors.
- Send a Word Doc, unless the listing specifies a PDF. Not all ATS can read PDFs. This is another procedure I had to change. If offered "either", do use a PDF.
- Do not use the Header as your Letterhead. ATS cannot read anything in the Header or Footer. That means that

you can put your Name and Number in the Header from Page 2 onward for the sake of the human reader later without affecting the ATS.

- Don't use Columns for formatting. ATS can't parse them and they turn the content into nonsense. Use Tabs to create the neat appearance of columns.
- No templates - keep it simple and use Word. No multi-colored page sections, or sideways lettering - especially of your name and contact information.
- Don't put your degree or qualification after your name. The ATS read it as a single word, so it can create nonsense.
- ATS likes to read your name by itself on the page. Put your phone number across from it, and then your job title, which should match the listing, on the next line.
- *Do* put your whole street address in your letterhead - they look for this.
- I hear ATS work better with a line of equal signs as section dividers, rather than fancy underlining, boxes or shading. It's a shame, but perhaps technology will improve over time and allow for more visually appealing customizing.

CHAPTER 15: INTRODUCTION TO ANALYZING A JOB LISTING

I will go into step-by-step detail about how I analyze and dissect each of my clients' job listings both to understand the full picture of the job, as well as find the repeated keywords and concepts in my upcoming book **"Understanding Job Listings: How to Customize your Resume and Cover Letter for Each Job."**

However, in the interim here are some tips to get you started.

Read the whole thing, including the company information which may be at the start or the end. Look for *repeated* words, including changes in tense of the same word (e.g.: manages, managing). You are especially looking for verbs as well as descriptors. Make notes. Count the repeats.

Look for the use of pronouns. A company that uses a lot of "we" and "our" often is less formal and likes to think of itself as a family and will be strong on teamwork and collaboration.

Notice what is missing from the job listing, especially larger concepts rather than picayune details of duties. For example, a team focused listing might not have anything about supervising others or controlling a budget in the duties. Therefore, it is futile, even damaging, to focus on those in your resume or cover letter.

You can save time by going to Jobscan at https://www.jobscan.co/ and entering by copy-and-paste your resume and the job listing, to get a report on the matching keywords. You are allowed a certain number of scans for free, before being invited to subscribe. Don't include the company information in the Jobscan copy-and-paste. Be aware that Jobscan is very literal, so it would view "report" and "reporting" as two different keywords. It misses some of the nuances that a human will notice from doing the analysis by hand.

But it is a good start.

Here's another ATS tip: once people cottoned on to how the ATS worked to count keywords, they started finding tricks to beat them, like copy-and-pasting the entire job listing at the end of the resume, or keyword loading with the font colored white. So now if your resume is at 100%, it will likely be red flagged. You should incorporate as many keywords and phrases as are an accurate reflection of your skills, but also use your own words. It's just like when SEO first became a thing, and people would write repetitive nonsense to rise in the search results, but now the bots are smart enough to know gibberish when they see it.

Perhaps of equal importance to discerning keywords, is analyzing the job listing to ensure that it is the job that you want. I had a client who wanted to apply to a vacant job at Pixar, as an entree into the company, with the hope of eventually being a producer. She had glanced superficially at the job and thought she could manage the general duties. She was an extrovert, gregarious, and loved the company culture.

However, on close inspection, from the very first paragraph it was clear to me that this job was not at all suited either to her qualifications, or her personality. They were looking for an introvert who loved data entry, whose delight would be sitting alone in a basement staring into the computer all day long, who was happy to report in writing rather than verbally if at all possible and thrived on predictability. In fact, they worded the listing very carefully to ensure that they were not inundated with filmmaking hopefuls, even to using a *different company description* from the rest of the creative and support jobs listed at the company.

Reading your prospective job listings with a pen in your hand is a very good idea.

Very best wishes for your job search and your career in the wonderful world of entertainment. Visit my website, http://WorkInProduction.com, for more information, tips, and interviews with many splendid filmmakers.

www.ingramcontent.com/pod-product-compliance
Lightning Source LLC
Chambersburg PA
CBHW070346220526
45467CB00001B/258